PERFECT PHRASES *for* LEADERSHIP DEVELOPMENT

Hundreds of Ready-to-Use Phrases for Guiding Employees to Reach the Next Level

Meryl Runion and Wendy Mack

McGraw Hill

New York Chicago San Francisco Lisbon London Madrid Mexico City
Milan New Delhi San Juan Seoul Singapore Sydney Toronto

The McGraw·Hill Companies

7 8 9 10 11 12 QVS/QVS 20 19 18 17 16

ISBN 978-0-07-175094-3
MHID 0-07-175094-0

Library of Congress Cataloging-in-Publication Data

Runion, Meryl.
Perfect phrases for leadership development : hundreds of ready-to-use phrases for guiding employees to reach the next level / by Meryl Runion, Wendy Mack.
p. cm.
ISBN 978-0-07-175094-3 (alk. paper)
1. Leadership. 2. Management. 3. Business communication. 4. Communication in management. I. Mack, Wendy. II. Title.

HD57.7.R863 2011
658.4'092014—dc22 2010029843

Interior design by Glyph International

This book is printed on acid-free paper.

Contents

Foreword

I am delighted to introduce you to this wonderful book from Meryl Runion, with my contributions. When I met Meryl she had already written five successful books, including *Perfect Phrases for Managers and Supervisors,* which was on my shelf, and she had a huge community of SpeakStrong fans. I was a bit awe-struck but put at ease by Meryl's generosity, spirit, and curiosity as well as our mutual love of knowledge and the outdoors.

Meryl and I hike weekly to trade ideas and share inspiration. On one of our hikes, Meryl mentioned she had an idea for a new *Perfect Phrases* book on developing emerging leaders. I stopped in my tracks and said, "Wow! The world needs that book!" My client organizations and organizations globally are on the verge of leadership crisis. As baby boomers retire, there are not enough people ready to move into their positions. Those that recognize this are actively creating and implementing succession planning programs and processes.

While succession planning is a step in the right direction, it won't be enough if the focus is simply on putting people into management roles. The senior executives I work with recognize that while they can promote managers, they need people who can truly lead. They see leading as being able to influence and inspire, to get things done even when you are not in charge, and to catalyze and create change.

The world of work is changing. Speed and constant connectivity are the norm. The control that accompanied leadership roles disappeared as information became available with the click of a button. Being a leader today is not about having followers who wait for you to tell them what to do and how to do it. It's about mobilizing energy and accelerating alignment so people are willing and able to take actions that further the interest of your organization . . . without waiting for direction.

Leadership communication is undergoing a significant shift. In a Leadership 3.0 world, leaders ask questions. We have conversations rather than issue commands. We listen more and talk less. We dialogue rather than delegate, demand, direct, and debate.

Meryl's New Dynamics of Communication and the phrasing recommendations are invaluable for anyone who wants to develop leaders who succeed in this new world of work. As you use the phrases to develop, encourage, and support others, you'll find yourself paying attention to and improving your own leadership skills.

While I am sure this book would have come to fruition without my enthusiasm and contributions, it has been great fun to be involved through its development.

So, read this book. Mark it up and refer back to it. Use the suggested phrases and develop your own. You do a great service to your organization by developing the next generation of dynamic leaders!

—Wendy Mack

Preface

The nature of leadership has changed dramatically in the twenty years Wendy and I have worked with leaders. That's why this book turned into resting grounds for outdated leadership concepts and a haven for Dynamic Leader practices.

This process evolved in the e-mails Wendy and I sent each other with our favorite leadership quotes and adages. We dashed off oldies but goodies and newly discovered gems, only to realize we needed to update them. For example, I sent Wendy the adage, "A leader is someone others choose to follow." I like how the saying captures choice over coercion. Yes, and Wendy reminded me that it's not about getting people to follow anymore. It's about getting them to engage. Yeah, I knew that. That adage went on my list of sayings to revise. An Internet search on the phrase, "a leader is someone who . . ." uncovered a hundred other adages, many useful, but none that captured the essence of leadership we witness emerging in today's work world and that we present here.

I responded to Wendy's offerings in much the same way. Every quote needed a tweak, caveat, or new dimension to make it viable for today's new Dynamic Leadership.

Dynamic Leaders Create Dynamic Leaders

Were we being picky? Yes, and we were also practicing what we teach here. We were being precise, expansive, and transformative. We took charge of the process, we challenged the status quo when the status quo seemed too small, and we innovated. We subjected all ideas to reconsideration. No concept was safe—whether it was an idea we cherished, the brainchild of someone we consider a mentor, or a newly encountered perspective that caught our attention. Instead of taking anything as a given—no matter how many times we had heard it or said it ourselves—we subjected it all to the scrutiny of our evolving vision of dynamic new leadership. We labored to clarify what it means to be a Dynamic Leader and to elevate the leadership development process to its highest level.

You face the same challenge we did—to take charge of your own process, challenge any assumption (status quo) you find in this book, and innovate to meet your specific leader development needs. Create your own definitions of what a Dynamic Leader is. Test them with other ideas and with reality. Draw your own conclusions so when someone asks you to fill in the sentence, "a Dynamic Leader is someone who . . ." you'll have a ready response that you can speak with conviction.

A Dynamic Leader Is Someone Who . . .

If a leader isn't best defined as someone others choose to follow, what is she or he? We say a Dynamic Leader primarily is someone who empowers others to lead.

That is what we aimed to do in this book.

—Meryl Runion

Acknowledgments

Every time I write acknowledgments for a book, I have more to acknowledge than I did in the previous book. That's because the Dynamic Leader style of thinking, communicating, and operating increasingly becomes my personal credo in deed as well as word. Every new writing endeavor is more of what I call a synocratic adventure. Each work includes more of the wisdom of great thinkers that I am blessed to be associated with.

I acknowledge my mentor and soul friend, Evan Hodkins. Every week we exchange ideas and liberate them from remaining vestiges of limitation and contention. Our dialogues are so synergetic that it's hard to know where my thinking stops and his starts. If he were not the great soul that he is, I would be concerned about sufficiently crediting him on every page I write because his influence touches each thought and word. For example, the term "synocratic adventure" in the first paragraph here originated with Evan. He made it abundantly clear that I am free to use anything that comes from our time together, with or without sharing credit. He puts it this way, "There's no ego on earth large enough to copyright this stuff." In true Dynamic Leader style, he delights in seeing what gets birthed from our association.

Then there's my coauthor, Wendy. If she hadn't almost turned cartwheels in the middle of Outpost Road with excitement when I shared the idea of this book, I might not have pursued it with such vigor. Our weekly hikes, where we discuss our ideas and our client experiences, added a relevancy to the ideas on these pages as, of course, did her informed input into the content. She is a true Dynamic Leader and a positive influence on every project she touches. She's dedicated and a visionary, and she delivers.

I had deeply insightful support from people who read my early draft and commented freely. Every time I review the manuscript I note a brilliant phrase Sharon Campbell recommended and delight in a concept that Lee Beaumont brought to my attention. Both were quite willing to suggest that at times I was giving only lip service to an idea or that my "Perfect Phrase" was what I—and they, knowing my work—call a Poison Phrase. Both were incredibly generous with their ideas, suggestions, and encouragement. Their input reflected clear awareness of what Dynamic Leadership is. (I recommend Lee's website, http://emotionalcompetency.com, for anyone who wants to explore a high level of discernment about the ideas on these pages.)

Then there's my team. Kris, Nathan, and Ashley rolled with all the fluctuations that working with me creates. Phyllis Khare catapulted me into the world of social media. She calls herself The Technology Cheerleader, but her cheerleading goes far beyond how to use the latest technology. There's my husband, Bob, who models integrity and clarity and knows how to lighten any situation by telling really dumb jokes.

To everyone who contributed in some way, I say thank you for helping me write a book that I fell in love with and for helping me to see new possibilities. That is a gift that has no measure.

Introduction

This book provides wording to effectively develop Dynamic Leaders at all levels for today's business environment. The phrases give concrete examples of what effective wording looks like and sounds like. As tempting as it is to use these phrases verbatim, you'll get the best results if you adapt instead of adopt them. Using static, cookie-cutter phrasing is counterproductive. After all, the *One Minute Manager* promptly led to *The Fifty-Nine Second Employee: How to Stay One Second Ahead of Your One Minute Manager*, which neutralized the perceived manipulative stock phrases managers learned. Let our phrasing guide you and spark your own creative communication. We don't want other authors to write books that arm people to resist manipulative tactics from leaders who misapply the phrases here. We offer tips to keep that from happening.

Adapt the Phrases to Guide Seasoned Leaders to Reach Their Next Level

Although the subtitle of this book refers to developing employees, you can use the phrases with anyone at any level who can use a more effective and Dynamic Leadership style—*if* you adapt them. Although many of the phrases assume a high level of commitment and engagement with emerging leaders, you can use them for general leadership development training, and informal leader development situations—*if* you adapt them.

A Caution About Questions

This book contains many questions. Questions take us on a quest for understanding. However, too often we ask questions manipulatively. Avoid putting your emerging leader on the defensive with questions that sound more like an interrogation than interest. Use questions to draw out rather than to test your emerging leader.

Perfect Phrases for Quick Reference

You can use this book as a quick reference for situations you face.

- Review relevant sections before you speak.
- Adapt the phrases to your need and personal style.
- Practice your phrases before you use them.
- After a conversation, review what you said, and determine ways you could have spoken more effectively.

Perfect Phrases as a Practical Dynamic Leader Development Course

A second approach is to use *Perfect Phrases* as a practical course in how to develop emerging leaders. Read *Perfect Phrases for Leadership Development* from cover to cover. Let it help you plan your leadership development approach. Then refer to sections as situations arise.

Let's Talk

Let's make our dialogue reciprocal. If your specific issue is not covered in this book, please e-mail me at MerylRunion@SpeakStrong.com or Wendy at Wendy@WendyMack.com. If you have a favorite phrase that you find useful, please forward it to us so we can add it to our collection of useful phrases.

Thanks for reading our book. Let us know how we have helped you or confused you and where we can engage with you in your leadership development process.

CHAPTER 1

What Is a Dynamic Leader?

Phrase books aren't explicitly about presenting new leader models or concepts. They're about translating concepts into words for success in specific situations. However, to direct readers to success, phrase book authors need working concepts of success to weave into their writing. Wendy and I developed and defined the Dynamic Leadership Style and honed the phrases in this book accordingly. The phrases here support you to speak as a Dynamic Leader yourself while you take your employees to the next level of emerging leadership.

If you are what author Jim Collins calls a Level 5 Leader, you're probably also a Dynamic Leader. If you have what author Stephen Covey calls interdependence, you're probably a Dynamic Leader. If you have what author Noel Tichy calls a teachable point of view, you're probably a Dynamic Leader. If psychiatrist Carl Jung would declare you to be individuated, or psychologist

Abraham Maslow would consider you to be self-actualized, you're probably a Dynamic Leader. If you see your own response as the greatest leverage you have in any situation, you're probably a Dynamic Leader. If you value these qualities and characteristics in employees, this is the book for you.

In the preface, a Dynamic Leader is defined as someone who empowers others to lead. That definition is expanded here:

- A Dynamic Leader has outgrown all forms of victimhood and tyranny, including manipulation and coercive power tactics, in favor of magnetic influence based on reciprocal engagement and confluent communication.
- A Dynamic Leader progressively clarifies and refines his or her own leadership philosophy and shares it eloquently with others.
- A Dynamic Leader serves organizational mission, vision, and values instead of personal power needs.
- A Dynamic Leader knows when to lead, when to manage, and when to stand down.
- A Dynamic Leader sees problems and obstacles as invitations to outgrow the perspectives that created them and to embrace higher perspectives to transform them.
- A Dynamic Leader uses Beginner's Mind to obtain fresh perspectives.
- A Dynamic Leader knows the stage a developing leader is at in his or her development process and engages that leader at the appropriate level.
- A Dynamic Leader empowers others by engaging their greatness more than by instruction.

- A Dynamic Leader progressively clarifies and refines a unique point of view by integrating input from self-reflection, study, mentoring, coaching, and feedback.
- A Dynamic Leader doesn't need the word *leader* in his or her title to take ownership of an area of influence.
- A Dynamic Leader measures personal leadership ability and that of others by the ability to empower others.

You can get a broader overview of what it means to be a Dynamic Leader by reviewing the Dynamic Leadership Index in Appendix A and online at www.speakstrong.com/leaderinventory.

Since every phrase in this book reflects what it means to be a Dynamic Leader and is developed to build Dynamic Leadership qualities in your employees, you can simply read on.

Leaders Need to Develop Leaders and Manage Succession

"I can go on vacation for two weeks and no one calls me with questions," Bob rejoiced. "My people can handle anything that happens." Bob is a leader who developed his employees into leaders. Bob empowered others.

He's also a leader who prepared for the possibility of his sudden departure. If Bob's uninterrupted vacations didn't get your attention, maybe this will. Bob left his position after seventeen years without creating a leadership vacuum.

The information and phrases here help you prepare for the future by developing leadership skills in employees, ensuring smooth succession transitions.

Succession Planning—It's Not Just for Senior Level Leaders Anymore

Although more than 80 percent of companies surveyed focus their succession planning efforts on the top three levels of their hierarchies, research shows a dramatic trend toward extending succession planning to retain high performers across all levels. They know they need consistency at every level.

The Immediate Need for Leadership at All Levels

Even when succession planning isn't an issue, this book fills an important need. Organizations require flexibility to adjust and adapt to a transforming business climate. We face too many internal and marketplace changes to be able to rely on precedent or attempt to control our organizations. Overworked leaders and executives can't adapt alone. We need employees who take charge, innovate, challenge outdated status quos, and implement change. The biggest differences between a successful company and an unsuccessful one can be how fast it responds, changes, and acts. Having leaders at all levels of the organization ready and empowered to make and implement decisions is key to that agility.

Exponential Resourcing

The dynamics that impel us to develop leadership potential and rely on the strengths of our employees also create a workforce that is increasingly receptive to stepping up to meet the challenge. With proper development, employees can think like mini-CEOs of their own domains, regardless of scope. They can envision what action is called for in the same way the CEO does. That's good news—and the good news doesn't stop there.

When employees shift from being followers to being leaders, the effect cascades. Partnership-based operational structures are becoming increasingly common, including worker-centered, self-organized, and self-designed teams. Books about leaders without titles fly off the shelves as leadership dynamics permeate every organizational level. De facto leadership becomes a norm.

Phrases That Empower Action

This book provides phrasing to transmute leadership from top down, command and control to dynamic partnership models. Our changing leader-development climate requires new tools to encourage, mentor, and coach employees at every level to be leaders who are empowered to act. Leaders need to develop leaders, and leaders need the approach and the phrases to do that.

Defining and Integrating Leadership and Management

A Dynamic Leader is someone who empowers others to lead. But what is the difference between a leader and a manager? We'll start by noting the tremendous confusion on the topic in the literature and workplace.

Flawed Thinking in the Leadership-Management Dialogue

In 1985, authors Warren Bennis and Burt Nanus claimed in their book *Leaders: The Strategies for Taking Charge,* "Managers are people who do things right and leaders are people who do the right thing." The catchphrase became a cliché and source of confusion.

First, the assertion created a false dichotomy that suggests that not only are the functions of leadership and management distinct, but they are in opposition to one another. To many, it implied that managers don't do the right thing and leaders don't do things right.

Second, the phrase distinguished managers from leaders. It is more accurate to distinguish management *activities* from leadership *activities*. In the real world, leaders also manage, managers also lead, and even nonleaders and nonmanagers both lead and manage (which is why leadership development is needed at all levels).

Third, the claim incited a valuation of one function over the other, with leadership generally winning favor over management. As a result, leadership training largely became held in higher regard than management training—although both authors get invited to provide "leadership training" that includes more management training content than leadership development.

This book avoids the false dichotomy between leadership and management, focuses on management and leadership activities instead of roles, and addresses the integration of both. We refer to the distinction between the activities in more detail in our phrases and in the appendices.

It Takes Leadership *and* Management Skills to Develop a Dynamic Leader

Leadership activities emphasize visioning, and management activities emphasize execution.

Each business situation is unique and calls for selecting from a broad set of skills. Leadership development involves blending both kinds of activities and guiding emerging leaders to have the appropriate mix of each. The phrases in this book cultivate leadership qualities at every level in ways that integrate with, rather than usurp, management activities and other forms of action and without creating a false dichotomy.

The Role of the Coach/Mentor in Developing Emerging Leaders

Just as in sports the coach never takes the field, the place for mentoring leaders is alongside an emerging leader, not in front. Dynamic Leaders coach to turn emerging leaders toward challenges and opportunities. If we're not careful, we'll turn the emerging leader toward *us*, instead. We coach to help emerging leaders recognize and take ownership of the full potential of their positions in the context of the larger organization. If we're not careful, we'll inadvertently put ourselves between them and that potential. We coach to help emerging leaders find their own internal resilience and resources, not to make them dependent on ours.

If we succeed, our emerging leaders leave our sides to guide other emerging leaders.

Be Wary of Cookie-Cutter Techniques

Avoid collecting prefabricated cookie-cutter techniques to perform on others. We "stay in relationship" with those we develop and watch out for any tendency to objectify them. This caution is particularly important here. Used unconsciously, scripted phrases replace our own thought processes and depersonalize communication. Used properly, they inspire and personalize our own thought processes. Personalize every phrase you select.

Let Yourself Be Transformed Too

We empower emerging leaders when we let go of any indication that we have all the answers and allow ourselves to be genuinely influenced. Mutual dialogue creates mutual learning. When we receive and acknowledge that learning, we move emerging leaders one step closer to their Dynamic Leadership potential. We also get the advantage of their wisdom and perspectives.

Integrate Management with Leader Development with Emerging Leaders You Manage

When our emerging leaders report to us, we're not just concerned about thought and skill development, we also need to hold our emerging leaders accountable for results. Leader development does not supersede the need for bottom-line considerations. The two roles conflict if we don't integrate them. The phrases in this book differentiate and communicate both roles.

Strike the Balance

Leadership development is an art, not a science. Just as doctors *practice* medicine and lawyers *practice* law, we also *practice* leader development. At times we will overdirect and need to back off. Other times we'll be too vague and need to be more concrete. Sometimes we'll ask too much. Other times we'll ask too little. And there will be times when we strike the perfect balance. The phrases in the chapters that follow empower Dynamic Leaders to strike that balance as often as possible.

The Four Stages of Emerging Leader Empowerment

Dynamic Leaders empower others to lead based on their skills, experiences, and abilities. Emerging leaders develop in dynamic, not linear, stages. A new project or topic changes the stage we work at. We—and our emerging leaders—must adapt from moment to moment. Track where your emerging leader is in each stage of his or her development and adapt your phrases to that level.

- **Exploratory:** The exploratory stage starts with the idea we could go anywhere together. Even if you have clear direction, at the beginning of this stage, downgrade those ideas into possibilities among other options that emerge from your interactions. Invite Beginner's Mind (the eagerness and openness that beginners often display) and mine fresh concepts without expectation.
- **Foundational:** In the foundational stage, Dynamic Leaders emphasize skills and knowledge on which to base higher levels of leadership. This might involve asking someone with great potential to do frontline tasks, not because that's all we think they can do, but because those activities provide a basis for future leadership responsibilities. A cleaning company that requires executives to work for a while as janitors applies this principle.
- **Guided Autonomy:** As emerging leaders develop skills and knowledge, we encourage decisiveness. Initially we'll ask them to walk us through their decision-making processes to uncover assumptions, flaws, and strengths

in thinking. We gradually invite emerging leaders to call audibles—make decisions to change directions based on how events unfold. (See "The New Dynamics of Communication" later in this chapter.) We follow up on those calls by debriefing decisions in later meetings and offering support and insight.

- **Autonomy:** At the autonomy stage, emerging leaders independently implement their own projects and responsibilities. We make ourselves available as resources. We have a high degree of synergy and invite them to dialogue with us about our own important decisions. At this stage, Dynamic Leaders ask for similar input as in the exploratory stage, but with a different purpose. Our new intentions are to (1) seek the wisdom and insight of someone who has developed a foundation and has become an independent thought leader, (2) experience the synergetic thinking this kind of collaboration affords, and (3) give the emerging leader opportunities to see and affect the organization from our level.

Discern the Stage

The stages of empowerment are scope and role specific and not an absolute attribute of the emerging leader at any point. Developing leaders can quickly reach the autonomous leader in areas where they have substantial previous experience but move more slowly and persist longer at prior stages in areas they are less familiar with. We hold our emerging leaders back if we don't grant autonomy when they're ready for it, and we frustrate them if we move them forward too quickly.

We wrote the phrases in this book to provide the perfect words you need at every stage of leader development.

Energy and Alignment: Two Dynamic Leadership Essentials

Whether we're moving an entire organization or a single emerging leader forward, our phrases need to create and maintain alignment and mobilize energy for change.

We Need Both Alignment and Energy

Energy fuels action, sparks innovation, and makes things happen. As mentors/coaches, a pivotal part of our jobs is to identify and tap into what motivates and energizes others to want to become leaders. But energy without alignment is chaos. If our emerging leaders are enthusiastic about their own ideas and energized about putting them into place, but we lack common focus, direction, and coordination, it can feel like herding cats.

Alignment means we move toward shared vision and goals with our actions focused and coordinated. Alignment means having a common agenda or "being on the same page."

While we need alignment for results, Dynamic Leaders find that alignment that is too rigid results in compliance or obedience and ultimately undermines energy. Our aligned emerging leaders may know what we expect but not really care. Rigid alignment could inhibit innovative suggestions and impede the ability to react to a sudden change that throws a plan off course. Dynamic Leaders (and our phrases) aim for Energized Alignment,™ a term created by coauthor Wendy Mack that integrates the qualities of energy and alignment.

How Dynamic Leaders Ignite Energy

Dynamic Leaders ignite energy by creating a clear vision of the end, including clear benefits. A journey is much easier when the travelers know where they are going and why.

We ignite energy when we both embrace the insight Beginner's Mind offers and create situations to take seasoned thinking back to Beginner's Mind for fresh perspective. Beginner's Mind is an emerging leader's key asset, and it is important for him or her to know we value that freshness.

How Dynamic Leaders Create Alignment

We create alignment when we redirect misaligned efforts rather than condemn them. Redirection keeps the forward momentum of the emerging leader's actions while guiding that person in a direction that coordinates his or her innovations with existing obligations.

We create alignment when we collaborate with emerging leaders to create discernment filters or decision criteria to evaluate situations. Those filters empower emerging leaders to be more autonomous with the confidence that their decisions complement rather than conflict with other efforts.

Balancing Two Potentially Oppositional Values

Energy and alignment may seem oppositional at times. Whether we are leading a major organizational change initiative or leading our emerging leaders into their full potential as leaders, it is worth the effort it takes to find the balance.

The New Dynamics of Communication

Women, Gen Y, social media, and globalization change the way we relate, influence, and succeed. They change the nature of power.

The phrases here apply contemporary influence principles that I call the New Dynamics of Communication. We include a brief introduction to the New Dynamics in the section that follows. I go into more detail in my book, *Perfect Phrases for Managers and Supervisors,* and at my website, www.speakstrong.com.

New Communication Dynamic #1: Be Gracefully Assertive

Say what you mean, and mean what you say without being mean when you say it. The 1980s brought about a rise in "power talk" through assertiveness training. The emphasis was on authority and "telling it like it is." The current communication trends add grace to the assertive equation, and the trend moves away from coercive power toward magnetic pull. New Dynamic Leaders may have less control, but they do have more influence than old rule communicators.

New Communication Dynamic #2: Personalize

The 1980s and early 1990s emphasized impersonal objectivity. Successful leaders were expected to hide their humanity and avoid bringing their personalities and styles into play. The saying "it's business, it's not personal" dismissed the relationship aspect of communication. We had "human resources" instead of people working for us. Now, Dynamic Leaders use business communication language that is increasingly personalized, engaged, and conversational.

New Communication Dynamic #3: State Concisely

Whether we love or hate the microblogging marvel Twitter, we can't ignore it. It changes the world we live in. Twitter and similar sites shape and reflect the nature of today's workforce—even beyond those who use it. Communication is increasingly about being precise, concise, and simple without being simplistic. Dynamic Leaders can develop this succinctness by learning to speak in sound bites and avoiding the temptation to pontificate. Pithy words get heard. Anything we communicate that doesn't add to a message detracts from it—and doesn't compete with the latest text message or Twitter post.

New Communication Dynamic #4: Synergize

The workplace isn't a democracy where the majority rules—it is a synergetic setting where all involved contribute to outcome. That means we come to the playing field and engage; invite collaboration and partner with the people we mentor, lead, and coach; and alchemize differences. Find the synergy between individual natures within each team, group, and unit.

New Communication Dynamic #5: Dynamize

The social dynamics of our culture demand dynamic momentum. We "dynamize" our communication by using language and communication that impels (not compels) forward thinking, speaking, and action.

The New Dynamics keep our communications up-to-date. The phrases in this book apply their contemporary influence principles.

Tips to Customize Communication to Each Emerging Leader

Dynamic Leaders adapt to the styles of the leaders they seek to empower. There's a marvelous fable called "Animal School" in which different animals—ducks, eagles, and squirrels—go through the same educational process and are evaluated equally on such skills as climbing, swimming, and flying. Expecting everyone to fit into the same template is counterproductive. Our first step in customizing our communication to each emerging leader is to recognize the value of using an individualized approach. Once we know why we bother customizing our communication, we can apply several resources to do that.

- **Mine your experiences.** What approach works or has worked with you? How could you apply what worked with you to your emerging leader? Go inward to walk in their shoes.
- **Ask emerging leaders.** A glaringly obvious but often overlooked way to customize our approach is to ask emerging leaders what works for them. Our emerging leaders can be an excellent resource for customizing our leader development communication . . . if we take the initiative to ask.
- **Watch for responses.** Notice what lights an emerging leader's fire. Monitor responses for the level of enthusiasm.

Observe your own energy, too. Energy indicates we're on to something.

- **Note emerging leader preferred communication modalities.** How do our emerging leaders communicate with each other? Orally? Written? Face-to-face? Do they use texting, e-mail, or Facebook? Consider embracing their favored modality. If we assume the emerging leader should communicate with us through our favored modality, we miss an opportunity to expand our own horizons by adjusting to theirs.
- **Create communication agreements.** Formal communication agreements help Dynamic Leaders keep the flow smooth and effective. Establish agreements collaboratively and follow the cues presented here to see how you want to adapt them. Some areas for agreements are how to update each other, how often to meet, and which activities require input and which don't. My team and I created a list of codes for e-mail subject lines and organization. These codes increased our efficiency and reduced our frustration. Our communication covenant affirms how we show up for each other.
- **Keep it dynamic.** Every relationship needs to be allowed to shift and grow. When things seem to get static, shift your approach.

CHAPTER 2

Perfect Phrases to Set the Stage

A Dynamic Leader develops leaders by entering into a partnership-style relationship. It is a collaboration of peers. Every partnership requires and deserves proper preparation and kickoff. It's a little like a marriage. We want to commit to the same thing.

That's why we set the stage to start. We enter our partnership relationship clearly understanding what we're getting into, who is getting into it with us, and what our purpose is. We also make sure the emerging leader is playing by the same understandings, goals, and expectations. We set the stage by getting to know each other, developing a structure for the process, formalizing and affirming understandings, and celebrating and confirming the new relationship.

Perfect Phrases to Discover the Emerging Leader's Style, Objectives, and Potential

These phrases illuminate your emerging leader's style, goals, objectives, and potential.

- What does being an emerging leader mean to you?
- What do you see as the difference between a Dynamic Leadership Style and a more traditional style? What do you prefer about each?
- If you could study leadership with anyone in the world, other than me, with whom would you study?
- What is the most masterful example of great leadership you can think of? What made it great?
- What is your greatest leadership asset?
- Give an example of leadership that you think was misguided. What was wrong with it?
- Give a specific example about a time when you were in (took) a leadership role.
    - What did you do well?
    - What qualities would you have liked to have had that you lacked?
    - What qualities did you display that contributed to your success?
    - Do you consistently display those qualities?
- Why are you interested in developing as a leader?
- Why do you want to develop as a leader with me?
- Imagine you are the CEO now. What will you do first?

- If you were your senior leader now, what would you do first?
  - Describe what your first thirty days would look like.
- What attracts you to being a leader?
- How does being a leader benefit you?

Perfect Phrases to Develop Measurements of Success as Dynamic Leaders

These phrases help you collaborate with your emerging leader about how to measure results. They create a standard and vision to aspire to.

- I'd like you to complete a leadership index so we'll have a baseline to track your development. (See Appendix A and www.speakstrong.com/leaderinventory/.)
- The best goals are ones we collaborate on.
- What area would you like to develop? How can we define success in that area?
- Imagine it's a year from now and you're evaluating your success. What's different?
- I'd like to see you develop in the area of ________. Does that sound like a reasonable target?
  - What would be a good target?
  - How does the wording sound to you? Can we improve it?
  - How will we measure that?

- I'd like your direct reports to complete their own leadership indexes since one of the best measures of a leader is how much they develop other leaders.
- Let's complete the leadership index each as well. We'll monitor our progress. How should we measure my contribution to this partnership?

Perfect Phrases to Communicate What It Means to Be an Emerging Dynamic Leader

These phrases clarify what being an emerging leader is, what it means, and what it doesn't mean. They provide the frame for the leader development process.

- We're investing in developing your leadership skills because we value you and believe you are capable of operating at the most senior levels.
- Being an emerging leader is a little like riding a bike with training wheels. I guide, but I don't ride the bike for you.
- I realize "leader" isn't in your title. It doesn't need to be. Dynamic Leadership is a style more than a position.
- We'll be moving you toward increasing leadership responsibilities. It's not an overnight transformation. It's a gradual process. It's not a linear road but an exploration.
- There isn't a single right way to be a leader. Being an emerging leader is about finding *your* best way.

- I'm not going to give you a leadership model. I want you to develop your own. I'm happy to share mine with you. Yours will be some blend of mine, other leaders' styles, and your own original ideas.
- What does being an emerging leader mean to you?
- This relationship is to develop your ability to think like a CEO. I want you to think like the CEO of your domain and that includes thinking like the CEO of our leader development partnership.
- As an emerging leader, you might feel you are in over your head at times. If we gave you only things you already know how to do, you wouldn't learn. But I'm here to keep you from drowning. Don't wait to go under a few times before you ask for help.

Perfect Phrases to Dispel Preconceptions and Address Misperceptions About Dynamic Leadership

These phrases explore preconceptions and misperceptions about what being a leader means. They update leadership concepts to a Dynamic Leadership model.

- A lot of people think you have to be born a leader. That might be true if there was only one good leadership style. But there isn't.
- Fill this in. A leader is someone who ___________.

- → We don't have to have a title or other formal positional power to lead. Sure, it helps, but it's not the only factor in being able to lead. It isn't even the most important factor.
- → Some people think coercion is leadership. When you think about it, any kind of pushing or pulling is the opposite of leading.
- → Leading isn't about personal wins. It isn't about treating other people as objects. It isn't about intellectual intimidation and bullying. It's about what serves the mission, vision, and values. That requires collaboration.
- → This is not your father's leadership development program. We're developing dynamic, transformational leadership. We're developing the willingness and ability to champion changing the rules of the game when the old rules hold us back and need changing.
- → When I first developed leadership skills, I thought I needed to have all the answers. I was wrong. Being a leader doesn't mean having all the answers, and being an emerging leader is more about finding good questions than having answers.
- → A lot of people think leaders need to be ________ (charismatic, outgoing, etc.). There are lots of ways to lead, and many of them don't require those qualities.
- → Being a leader doesn't mean everyone else is a follower. It means you draw out the possibilities all around you.
- → I'll coach and I'll test, but I won't direct. Leadership isn't telling you what to do. It's exploring and evaluating possibilities to guide what you do.

- Think of me as a mirror held up to reflect your thinking and help you decide—is this the best choice?
- Do you see me holding on to old leadership ideas in how I lead? Call me on it when you do.

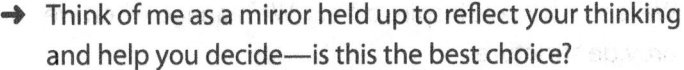

Perfect Phrases to Distinguish Between and to Balance Leadership and Management

These phrases guide the emerging leader to balance management activities with leadership activities.

- Ideas and execution go hand in hand. You don't need to be able to personally implement ideas in order for them to be good ones, but you do need to be realistic about what their execution would involve.
- Leaders sometimes also need to act as dynamic managers to create stability and efficiency through budgeting, planning, staffing, scheduling, and problem solving.
- Great leaders are great managers when they need to be. Great managers are great leaders when they need to be. And we all need to know how to balance both functions.
- We lead when we set a direction. We manage when we carry out that direction.
- We lead when we work with ideas and people. We manage when we work with processes for people to implement. Which are you focusing on now?
- We lead when we create a vision. We manage when we create a plan.

- We lead when we inspire others. We manage when we provide structure.
- We lead when we envision, propose, and create change. We manage when we organize how the change will be implemented.
- We lead when we see what could be. We manage when we deliver what is and what leadership decided will be.
- We lead when we originate initiatives. We manage when we make the initiatives happen.
- We lead when we develop other leaders. We manage when we take action to make sure the leadership development process moves smoothly.
- I expect you to lead some in our leader development process and to manage some. It will be a dynamic process.
- Are you thinking like a leader or a manager right now? One isn't inherently better, but it's good to know which it is.
- How would you define the difference between leadership activities and management activities?

Perfect Phrases to Share Your Personal Leadership Philosophy

What is unique about your personal leadership philosophy? What lessons has your experience taught you about leadership that could be useful to the emerging leaders you are developing? By sharing your own experience, you personalize the process, give your emerging leader the benefit of your own experience, and provide insight into your own frame of reference.

- I'll share my leadership philosophy with you to help you define yours.
- I used to think leadership meant ____________. Now I see it as being more about ____________.
- My leadership style is best summed up as ____________.
- A good leader always ____________. A great leader always ____________.
- The difference between a good leader and a great leader is ____________.
- A lot of people think leadership means ____________ (e.g., being authoritative). I think leadership means ____________ (e.g., being influential).
- One of the biggest misunderstandings I find people have about leadership is ____________.
- My role model of excellent leadership is ____________ (name).
- I know someone is a leadership natural when I observe ____________.
- My definition of a leader is someone who ____________.
- My leadership philosophy has evolved over time from ________ to ________. Some of the books (people, experiences, etc.) that helped me do that are ____________.

Perfect Phrases to Guide Emerging Leaders to Develop Their Personal Leadership Philosophies

These phrases support our emerging leaders to develop their leadership styles without being imitations of us.

- How would you define your leadership philosophy?
- I'll share my leadership philosophy but consider this only one of many sources. I'm asking you to develop your own.
- How has your definition of "leadership" evolved through the years?
- What do you see as the difference between a good leader and a great one?
- What qualities do you think are most important in leadership?
- Fill in the blank. A leader is someone who ________.
- Tell me something about your leadership philosophy that you think would surprise me.
- What books about leadership inspire you?
- Name some leaders you admire.
  - What do you admire about how they lead?
  - How is your personal leadership philosophy different from theirs?
- How would you say your personal leadership philosophy is different from mine?

Perfect Phrases to Invite Reverse Mentoring and Mutual Development

These phrases invite the emerging leader to look for teaching opportunities as well as learning opportunities in the leadership development process.

- This is a mutual development relationship. If you have ideas or think of things you believe I need to know, I want to hear them.
- The best teachers say that they learn as much from their students as they teach. I plan to learn from you while you learn from me.
- I'm not here to give you all the answers. I'm here to help you find your own and for you to help me find better answers, too.
- What am I not seeing that you do?
- What do you know that you think I should know?
- Please share with me (1) an overview of the work you are doing, (2) what is going well that needs to be continued, (3) what is not going well and needs to be changed, and (4) anything else you find relevant to our working together.
- Be on the lookout for teaching opportunities as well as learning opportunities.
- I'd like feedback, and I don't want you to say what you think I want to hear. I do ask you to be gracefully assertive in your word choice, however.

- → What skills do you think I need to develop that I haven't?
- → If there's something I don't see or some information I don't have, please share it with me.
- → I've been at this longer, so I might have more to share with you for a while. Or, I might not. Don't let my experience overshadow yours.
- → I want to learn as much as you do here.
- → Sometimes I get so excited about my own ideas that I forget to stay open to yours. If my attempts to be helpful seem intrusive to you, let me know.
- → If I'm teaching when I should be listening and learning, I want you to tell me.
- → I want us to talk in an interactive way so everyone gets smarter.
- → Your advice helps me in three ways. I'll find out what you know, I'll learn some things, and I'll find out where I can support you.
- → I expect to be a lot smarter after our meeting than I was before.

Perfect Phrases to Establish Guidelines and Expectations of Your Mentoring and Coaching Relationships

These phrases establish an understanding of our mutual commitment level and expectations so we don't get deep into a partnership only to discover that someone we invested ourselves in deeply doesn't share our level of commitment.

- How do you anticipate us working together?
- What kind of commitment do you envision us making to each other and the leader development process?
- We need the same level of commitment to this process. Are we going for a little change or a huge transformation? I'm in, fully committed to your complete success and transformation, and my own in the process, if you are.
- The success of this relationship requires commitment. The company is committing to us, I'm committing to you, and you're committing to me. But really, we're all committing to your potential and success.
- We will have competing priorities. Let's anticipate what we're likely to face and what we can realistically commit to.
- There's not a standard formula for what we're doing. It's what we create. We can create any guidelines and structures we want, but we do need to decide on a structure and honor it until we renegotiate something else.
- I expect you to risk making tough decisions. Are you in?

- When you make a mistake, we'll both learn from it by working through the consequences. That way you'll really grow—and so will I.
- If we make a mistake, let's agree to admit it. If one of us admits a mistake, let's agree to both learn from it.
- We could do this in a halfhearted way and slide through the program. I say we give it our very best and get everything we can out of it.
- "Staying in relationship" means we interact and work through issues and challenges. When a problem occurs, we move toward the problem to solve it instead of away from it to ignore it.
- I have two roles here. I manage you, and I am here to help develop your leadership skills. At times those roles will conflict. If you find that they do, or you're confused about which role I'm speaking from, let me know.
- We are likely to have times when we don't see eye to eye. When that happens, we need to "stay in relationship" and show up for each other as we say we will. Agreed?
- Whatever structure we decide on and whatever else we commit to, one thing I want us to commit to 100 percent is to do what we say we will. If life interferes and makes it impossible, we'll address it and renegotiate rather than ever letting it slide.

Perfect Phrases to Establish Communication Standards

These phrases create communication standards to minimize misunderstanding.

- Communication standards are like agreeing to the rules of a pickup basketball game before we start. It ensures we're playing the same game the same way.
- What communication standards would you like us to establish?
- The communication standard I insist on is candor (or your favored standard).
- I might not realize that I haven't explained something completely. If you are missing important information, please ask.
- If you leave my office without understanding what I said, it's your responsibility. If things are unclear, stay and insist I clarify.
- Sometimes we can use the same word but have a different intent or meaning. If it seems to either of us that we are not really communicating, let's agree to stop and find out where it went wrong.
- How often would you like to meet?
- I'd like us to meet ________ (weekly, monthly) and update each other ________ (frequency) in between. Does this sound like the right amount of time to you?

- When I call or e-mail, I'd like a response within twenty-four hours, even if it's just to say when you'll be able to get back to me. I'll commit to the same. Can you agree to that?
- When we e-mail each other, let's make a point to bullet separate points, mark questions, and keep the subject line current to the topic.
- If you wonder if you should or shouldn't communicate something to me, go ahead and communicate.
- Let's agree to talk about what we want more than what we don't want—and what would work more than what isn't working.
- If we can't deliver on promises, let's offer our reasons but never give excuses. Agreed?
- What are your preferred technologies for communicating? Will you teach me how to use them effectively if I don't know them?

Perfect Phrases to Affirm Agreements

These phrases get the commitment we need to assure smooth interaction. They also give us a standard to compare behavior to should commitment to the process wane. (See Chapter 7 for phrases to address communication challenges and other issues.)

- We'll hold each other accountable for the things we agree to, but more than that, we'll *help* each other *be* accountable. Do you agree to that?

→ Do the guidelines work for you?

→ Is there anything that would keep you from honoring the guidelines?

→ How can the guidelines be improved?

→ Will you agree to let me know if we need to change and adapt the guidelines to make them work?

→ I commit to the guidelines as part of my commitment to you, your future in this organization, and our partnership. Do you?

→ Do you pledge to accept the challenge?

→ It's an honor to be working with you this way.

→ Let's create a document with our agreements and sign it. Then, let's celebrate by ___________.

CHAPTER 3

Perfect Phrases to Navigate the Empowerment Process

A Dynamic Leader relates to developing leaders at the appropriate level. If we relate at the wrong level, it can be overwhelming and stifling, appear condescending, or simply be unproductive.

This chapter includes phrases to communicate at each stage of the emerging leader's empowerment journey. Some areas of development call for different empowerment levels. These phrases help us find the balance between micromanaging the leadership development process, abdicating our own leadership role, and collaborating appropriately. You can read more about these stages in the section titled "The Four Stages of Emerging Leader Empowerment" in Chapter 1.

Perfect Phrases to Communicate, Stage One: Exploratory

The overriding objective of the exploratory stage is for us to get to know our emerging leaders and for them to get to know us and to explore the organization at a higher level. The phrases below include asking for input on things that are likely a bit beyond an emerging leader's reach. That uncovers emerging leaders' skills and limits, invites Beginner's Mind, and gives a sense of how they think without the influence of our ideas. It also gives our emerging leaders a focus that involves deep research that will familiarize them with the organization and operations.

➜ We're in the discovery process. It's a bit like a yard sale, class reunion, or blind date. If you stay open, you never know what you'll find.

➜ We're new at working together like this. I don't know what you know and what you don't. If I assume knowledge, don't pretend you have it. Let me know.

➜ In the exploratory stage, I'll ask you for input and ideas about major initiatives without providing much direction. I'll do this with four objectives: (1) to get a sense of your thinking without the influence of my ideas, (2) to give you a focus that involves research that will familiarize you with the organization (department, project, etc.), (3) to give me an understanding of your style by observing how you proceed so I can know how we can best work together, and (4) to be surprised by ideas I haven't considered.

➜ I want to explore how you think, what you know, where you're strong, and where you need more experience or training. To do that, I'll give you projects that might be beyond the scope of your expertise. You can't fail discovery, so just do what you can and ask for guidance where needed. Agreed?

- In our early weeks together, I'll be asking you to do things I don't expect you to know how to do. It's an exploration, not a pass-fail test.
- I'm going to ask questions you probably don't know the answers for. If you don't have an answer, let me know and then respond by telling me what you imagine you'd say if you *did* have one.
- Next time we meet, I'd like you to bring the details of a project that would grow business. Make it a serious proposal. If it shows promise, we might see how we can implement it. You can't get this wrong because we'll learn from whatever you bring.
- If you were CEO tomorrow, what would you do?
- Where do you think the organization needs to take a new direction?
- How would you improve quality here?
- What do you see as our best growth opportunities?
- What did you do to prepare for this meeting and be prepared for us to play as peers?
- What do you know that you suspect I don't?
- What skills would you suggest I need?
- If you were me and considering a project for you to start with, what would that project be?

Perfect Phrases to Communicate, Stage Two: Foundational

The overriding objective of the foundational stage is to provide experience and knowledge to give basis for higher levels of Dynamic Leadership. Some of the experiences we provide can seem elementary, such as a high-level hospital administrator spending several days at the clinic reception desk or a regional manager working on the factory floor. These phrases tie our communication into the overall development plan, so the emerging leader recognizes that an approach that could seem regressive is a step forward.

- If you've seen the TV show "Undercover Boss," you'll understand the value of what I'm going to ask you to do. I want you to ___________ (e.g., work on the shop floor for three days).
  - The value of this is ___________.
- We need to know what's going on with real customers in the real marketplace. To get that experience I'd like you to ___________.
- If a leader doesn't know what it's like on the front line, the leader can't lead. That's why I'm recommending you ___________.
- Leaders need to face reality as it is. That's why I'm asking you to ___________ (task) to find out what's really going on.
- I'm assigning you to ___________ (job, project). It may not seem like a step up, but it offers experience in ___________.

- → The road to leadership excellence has some bumps in it that require endurance.
- → The skills you'll acquire make it worth the sacrifice.
- → We're going to expand on your current skills and build new ones by __________.
- → Everyone can teach us something. I'd like you to __________ (activity) to learn what the experience can teach you.

Perfect Phrases to Communicate, Stage Three: Guided Autonomy

The overriding objective of the guided autonomy stage is for the emerging leader to learn to apply skills and knowledge with appropriate decisiveness. These phrases invite Dynamic Leadership protégées to walk us through their decision-making processes and uncover assumptions, flaws, and strengths in thinking as a step on their way toward autonomy. They allow the mentor and protégée to review decisions together after they have been implemented. (See Chapters 8 and 9 for more phrases to guide decisions.)

- → It's time for me to step back and be a resource and let you take on more autonomy here.
- → A month ago, I might have stared this conversation with my ideas. Now I'd like to start it with yours.
- → I'd like for us to create a different kind of information architecture where individuals at all levels have access

to information without having to rely on a cumbersome bureaucratic hierarchy. How could we start that process with you?

- That's a fair question, and I'd like for you to be able to make that kind of decision without having to go through me to get the information to make it. How can we arrange that?
- What do you think the best direction is in this situation?
  - How did you come to that conclusion?
  - What alternative decisions did you consider?
  - What values informed your decision?
- I'm used to directing the process more than is appropriate now. If I direct more than you need, tell me about it.
- Finish this sentence: After considering many alternatives, it became clear that our essential shared value is __________. That guided my decision to __________.
- This is a joint exploration. I want to wait until I hear what you think before I offer my observations.
- I'm not telling you that decision is wrong. I am asking you to convince me of why you think your decision is the best one.
- What objections do you imagine you would have to overcome to convince me or anyone else of that decision?
- It's not weak to ask for help. I'll coach you and support your decision, but I won't override your thinking.
- That decision seems to conflict with what you say you value because __________.

- Your greatest leverage in this situation is your own response. How could you respond differently and get a different result?
- That's a valid idea based on how we already do things. If you could disregard current thinking and do anything, what would you do?
- I can't answer that. Who do you think could?
- Let me tell you what I really like about that plan.

Perfect Phrases to Communicate, Stage Four: Autonomy

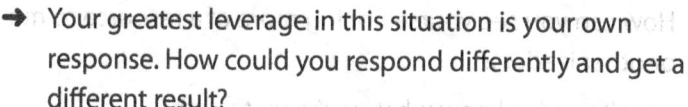

Let the synergy fly! At the autonomy stage, emerging leaders have their own projects and responsibilities that they implement independently. We offer ourselves as resources to them and invite them to dialogue with us about our own important decisions. The phrases at this stage access the wisdom and insight of a dynamic and independent thought leader. They also give the emerging leader opportunities to see and affect the organization from our levels.

- I believe we can both benefit from some level of ongoing collaboration. I invite that. I don't need to know what you're up to with ____________ (project), but I'm still here as a resource.
- Where do you see potential for you to be more autonomous?

- → How can you see yourself being more of a resource to me or other leaders?
- → I don't *need* to know what you're up to with ________ (project), but I'd sure *love* to find out what you're doing so I can learn a few things.
- → I have some ideas I'd like to noodle on with you.
- → I've got a white board here that is yours to fill with ideas you'd like input on.
- → Do you have time to brainstorm with me about an initiative I'm considering?
- → What would you do if you were me about ________?
- → How are you developing others to be Dynamic Leaders?
- → Who would benefit from working with you like we've worked together?
- → In the exploratory stage, I asked your input on major initiatives to get you thinking in that direction, to tap into your Beginner's Mind, and to discover how you think. Now I'm looking for your expertise, synergy, and inspiration.

Perfect Phrases to Communicate the Emerging Leader's Stage

The phrases below are progressively stage-specific. They give emerging leaders context so they can interpret our words knowing what level we are speaking from.

- Leader development is a process. We'll start by getting to know each other and brainstorming possibilities. We'll narrow the focus when we're ready and build a foundation of skills and experiences. Then we'll expand back out and build leader autonomy and decision making. We'll discuss what level we're working at as we communicate.
- We're in the early stages here and are exploring, not evaluating, what you know. Don't stress yourself out to get things perfect—just give it your best effort, and let me know what you don't know rather than try to get it all right.
- We're building a foundation of skills that will be invaluable once we shift the focus to decision making and autonomy.
- At this stage your foundational skills are strong. We're not ready for you to make transformational decisions on your own; I still want to be involved. But we are ready for you to do that with some guidance.
- Your decision-making skills are developed enough that I'm comfortable with you taking charge and updating me on a need-to-know basis. I do want to dialogue with you as a peer, however.

Perfect Phrases to Elevate and Adjust the Level of Empowerment

Our protégées might be ready for an empowerment level that is higher than where they currently operate. These phrases provide a nudge to elevate the empowerment stage as we see readiness. In the spirit of reverse mentoring, they also invite our developing leaders to comment when we can elevate our own level.

- ➜ Do you think you're operating at your highest capacity level here?
- ➜ We've focused on exploration long enough to know what skills and experience you need. I have ideas of how you can get that. We'll always keep exploring, but we're ready to narrow the focus and build the foundation for true transformational leadership.
- ➜ You've practically mastered the abilities and basic skills you need to work within your existing framework. It's time we focus more on how you can transform the framework with new initiatives and structures.
- ➜ You don't need me to guide you anymore. If you want to include me in your decision process, I'm here. If you want to share the results, you have my ear. You're ready to make transformational changes on your own—including when and how to involve me.
- ➜ How can we increase your empowerment level a notch?
- ➜ What ways do you see me ready to up my empowerment level a notch?

- I believe you are ready to break through and begin working at a new and higher level. Are you ready to move on, up and out?
- Can you convince me that this task is not worth doing?
  - Valid answers include (1) I agree it has to be done, but it is not the most important thing to be doing now; (2) I am not the best person to do that job because ___________, and I believe ___________ can better do it; and (3) I believe it is more important that I do ___________ because ___________.
  - If it isn't worth doing, what should you/we be doing instead?
- Are you above this? Why?
- I'd like to see you take on more autonomy with ___________ (project).
- Last month I would have wanted to be involved in this decision. I see you as ready to make it on your own now.

CHAPTER 4

Perfect Phrases to Ignite Energy and Enthusiasm

Energy and enthusiasm are essential to productivity. That's why we need to ignite energy in emerging leaders and guide them to ignite energy in others. The phrases in this chapter are designed to meet both needs. If we walk our talk and energize our emerging leaders, it will spill over. They will more naturally energize those they lead. If we add guidance about how they can energize their associates, we'll turn them into "energizing bunnies."

Some things that ignite energy are: clarifying benefits, creating vision, protecting confidence, talking about what works more than what doesn't work, infusing tasks with relevant meaning, and inviting others to take charge in areas where they might otherwise wait for direction.

Some things that undermine energy are pulling rank, reducing initiatives to numbers, and talking about problems and mistakes to the exclusion of successes and opportunities.

These phrases will energize your emerging leaders as they develop their ability to energizing others.

Perfect Phrases to Energize Emerging Leaders by Communicating the Benefits of Leadership Development

It's a useful cliché that everyone's favorite radio station is WII FM—"what's in it for me." If we question the destination, we will be uninspired on the journey. These phrases communicate the benefits of developing Dynamic Leadership qualities to keep your emerging leaders enthusiastic about the process.

- ➜ We're aspiring to new heights here. There may be times when we wonder why we left the old and familiar, but once we reach new peaks, we'll be glad about what we did.
- ➜ The reason why we know you can achieve these heights is ___________.
- ➜ What's in this for you?
- ➜ What "bennies" do you see in participating in leadership development?
- ➜ Many managers never make the transition into leadership. You might think the big boys have it. They haven't all gotten their arms wrapped around it. By the end of this journey, you'll have an edge few leaders have.
- ➜ It might sound trite, but what we're doing can transform you from being a subject of your fate into the creator of your destiny. What does that idea mean to you? What does it mean to you to be able to inspire others to develop that ability?

- ➜ Developing dynamic leadership skills is like being an architect instead of just a builder. We get to envision things that don't exist and make them happen. For example, ___________.
- ➜ This process can feel tedious at times, but once we've developed the skills, we come out transformed and ready to transform.
- ➜ I'm excited for you and about where this will take you—and where it will enable you to take others.
- ➜ This isn't just going to help your career, it's going to increase the fun of getting there.
- ➜ Leaders create the culture. There's something invigorating about that kind of influence.
- ➜ Dynamic Leaders may not control, but they have a lot of influence. That feels fabulous.

Perfect Phrases to Guide Developing Leaders to Energize Others Through Communicating Benefits

These phrases guide our emerging leaders to energize others by practicing the skill of communicating benefits.

- ➜ People want to know the *whys* before they get excited about *how*. The benefits are the *why*. How can you communicate benefits of ___________ (project) with the people you influence?

- I'm sure you've heard that everyone's favorite radio station is WII FM—"what's in it for me." People get excited by benefits. When you can energize people to action by communicating benefits, it's a huge step toward being a Dynamic Leader.
- You've told me what you're going to do and why. Now tell me the benefits for the people you want to influence. Can you use your reasons, or do you need to give them customized reasons they relate to better?
- If your associates don't seem energized, perhaps they don't understand the benefits to them. Are you listening to them enough to know what benefits will energize them?
- If your associates aren't motivated, perhaps you haven't communicated the benefits clearly enough.
- I can see why you want that. Why would they? How can you communicate that this is in their interest?
- People are more inspired on a journey if they have a clear picture of what they'll get by going. How can you express that in terms of what matters to them?
- Complete this sentence as if I'm the person you need to influence. "What's in it for you is ___________."
- Complete this sentence as if I'm the person you need to inspire. "This will benefit you by ___________."
- When we started this process, we spent a fair amount of time exploring the benefits for you in becoming a Dynamic Leader. It sounds to me like you need to do that with the people you want to motivate.

Perfect Phrases to Create Beginner's Mind

Because Beginner's Mind is one of the greatest gifts protégés bring to the table, the topic is included in this section on igniting energy. If we invite, develop, and apply the ideas that emerge from it, it will inspire our developing leaders. These phrases access the innocence of Beginner's Mind—even if our emerging leader has already been around the block a few times on his or her own. It also guides emerging leaders to invite Beginner's Mind in others.

- Do you have or know kids? Have they ever come up with ideas that were so amazing they floored you? That's Beginner's Mind. I want us both to think that way and for you to invite that quality in others.
- Dynamic Leaders are like kids at times. We want to examine everything to see if it's real or not. That's one reason why I don't dismiss any of your questions as "dumb" and encourage you not to judge or dismiss questions people ask you.
- Beginner's Mind has a child's curiosity and excitement about new information. There's an openness that is not looking to confirm what it "already knows." That's what makes it so useful. That's why Dynamic Leaders can learn from anyone and anyone can learn from us.
- If you could change anything around here, what would it be?
- Have you asked your associates what they would change?

- Ask me three deliberately "dumb" questions. Then invite people you influence to do the same.
- What would you suggest we do here if we couldn't fail? How could that actually happen?
- What would you suggest we do if everyone here was new and not invested in how things are?
- Let's not talk redecorating. Let's talk remodeling, rebuilding, relocating, or some other "re-volution" we haven't considered.
- Here, I have just handed you a magic wand. What are you going to do with it? Why?
- Here is my crystal ball. Please look into it and let me know what you see.
- Write a letter of resignation with an explanation of why. Say what was wrong with the company. Then give me a new vision.
  - What if we started from scratch?
  - What is your intuition telling you?
  - Here's an exercise for you. Ask the people you work with to imagine starting from scratch too.
- Pretend you're ___________ (a prominent individual such as Bill Gates or Michael Scott from "The Office") visiting here. Describe your perspective.
- We have an ever new business environment. Tell me what I'm not seeing.
- What are we assuming that might not be true?

- Let's imagine twenty possible ways to go about this.
- This week, look at everything that crosses your desk as an opportunity—particularly things that hit you wrong. Let me know at least three opportunities you see from unusual sources.
- Is there anything that we are doing that doesn't need doing? Please make a list.
- Are there any reports or other routine activities that are either useless or not as useful as they could be with some changes?
- Is there information that we should collect and use that we aren't?
- What business opportunities do you see that we don't?
- What business services or products do you see that you think will be obsolete in five years?
- What form do you see this business taking in five years? Next, ask your associates the same question and see how their ideas influence your answers.

Perfect Phrases to Get Employees to Let Go of the Past

When emerging leaders slip into past habits, these phrases reinforce the momentum to get them moving forward. Dynamic Leaders make the process reciprocal by inviting emerging leaders to note when we too slip into old habits. Additionally, we guide emerging leaders to lead others to let go of the past.

- Referring to the departments by their old names keeps us stuck in the past and sets a bad example for the rest of the organization. It's difficult to change old habits, I know, but I'll call your attention to it every time you do that.
- I've called the ________ (new department name) department the ________ (old department name) for thirty years. When you catch me doing that, please point it out to me. Changes like that require reworking a lot of old habits, and I could use your help with some of mine.
- We've updated those procedures. The old ones may still work for us, but as Dynamic Leaders we need to follow the new ways.
- Our job is to lead people to success. If they're going down a path where that can't happen, it's our job to find or create a new path.
- The past feels stable, but it's not. We're sacrificing the familiarity of the past for the opportunity of the future.
- Let me know when—I say *when* instead of *if* because it will happen—I sound stuck in the past. Whether you think it's just my word choice, a habit, or me being really out of touch, I want to hear about it.
- Why do I/you/your associates hold so firmly on to the past?
- What value do I/you/your associates still see in that past?
- Do the circumstances that caused us/them to do that in the past still exist in the present?
    - What does that tell us to do now?

- It sounds like the people you are learning to lead are holding on to the past. When they slip into old habits, find out why so you can motivate them to stay current or even get ahead of the curve.
- What could you say to your associates to inspire them to let go of the past?
- The best way to inspire people to let go of the past is to create a compelling picture of the future. What could you say or do that would inspire people to look ahead instead of back?

Perfect Phrases to Build Confidence

It's always a bit scary to expand in scope or responsibility. These energizing phrases build confidence while avoiding pandering. They also guide emerging leaders to consider building others' confidence as part of operating at the next level.

- As "they" say, the best way to eat an elephant is one bite at a time. Every journey begins with a single step. That's how we're going to develop your leadership skills.
- We're investing in developing your leadership skills because we value you and believe you are capable of operating at a senior (higher) level.
- Are there aspects of this that frighten or concern you that we can alleviate?

- I know you can do it. I trusted you from the start because ________.
- It says a lot about you that we're investing in your career and development.
- I like the way you ________.
- We, ________ (names and titles), selected you for this development because of your great work. We also agree your best work is ahead of you.
- I was telling ______ how I liked the way you ________.
- It's clear to me that you have tremendous untapped skills. Part of our mission is to figure out the best way to use them.
- Let's start with some goals we know you can reach.
- You and I wouldn't be doing this if we didn't see the potential in you.
- Don't worry about having all the answers. If you had everything figured out already, we wouldn't be here. Actually, none of us do.
- ______ (name) told me that you ________ (sincere compliment).
- I'm impressed by your work, and by you. I look forward to seeing just how great your influence can become.
- It sounds like a few of the people you work with are lacking the confidence they need to do their best work. How could you build their confidence?

- I sense you don't trust some of your associates to do the job. I expect they sense it too. What can you do to get confidence in them so you can build confidence in them?
- One of the things I've had to examine in my leadership role is ways I would undermine the confidence of people I wanted to influence. How might you be doing that?
- I'm hearing a lot about what your people are doing wrong. Might they be hearing too much about failures and not enough about successes? Is there a way you can shift the focus to energize them more?

Perfect Phrases to Infuse Tasks with Meaning

Many people consider easy, or "menial," tasks "beneath them." Dynamic Leaders know better and help emerging leaders understand that these tasks can teach them something important and be essential to the success of a bigger mission. These phrases tie immediate activities to the big picture to create meaning. They also charge emerging leaders to infuse meaning in their associates' tasks.

- If you don't know the proverb about how "for want of a nail . . . the kingdom was lost," read it. If you ever think what you're doing isn't important, that proverb will remind you what an enormous difference the smallest thing can make.

- Why is this task meaningful to you?
- You seem disengaged from (bored by, unenthused by, bothered by, uninspired by) this task. Are you? Why?
- What do you see as the greatest purpose of this task?
- This process is important for the future of our organization because ___________.
- This task is an important step in getting you fit for the future because ___________.
- These projects will help you fit in on a global basis by ___________.
- What we do here will help our mission by ___________.
- This project will help our vision by ___________. It's important that you understand that and that you help others understand how it ties into our vision.
- This activity reflects our values because ___________.
- If we do this well, it will make a huge difference for our company.
- I know you value _______ (diversity, efficiency, collaboration, etc.). What we're doing here will help that by ___________.
- It may seem like an insignificant activity, but it will build your greatness by ___________.
- It's a small step, but every step gets us closer.
- Once you've completed ___________ (task) you'll have developed ___________ (leadership skill).

- Here's a challenge for you. I'd like you to take a day to consider the importance of the jobs of everyone in your sphere of influence, and take another day letting them know why what they do is meaningful.
- Do you see how your associates' activities fit into the big picture? Part of your leadership role is to help them see it so they can experience what they do as more meaningful.

CHAPTER 5

Perfect Phrases to Create Alignment

It's great to see our people energized, but are they aligned? If a developing leader enthusiastically does something that opposes the mission, vision, and values of the organization or the leader development partnership, it sure isn't an effective use of his or her time. Dynamic Leaders create alignment with developing leaders and also guide developing leaders to create alignment in their areas of influence.

We and our developing leaders create alignment by keeping the mission, vision, and values relevant. This chapter provides phrases to channel energy in productive directions that create alignment and guide emerging leaders to channel efforts in productive directions. The mission remains a constant to guide dynamic action.

We and our developing leaders create alignment when we make it easy for others to present their ideas, questions, and concerns and otherwise be heard as well as when we assimilate and apply what they suggest. We create alignment when we ourselves consistently act in alignment with our stated direction and existing obligations.

We and our developing leaders undermine alignment when we have an agenda we don't articulate. People will feel set up and find themselves trying to align with what they imagine we want from them. We undermine alignment when we lack clarity or force conclusions before reaching clarity. Ambiguity is a part of any new initiative, and Dynamic Leaders need to carefully manage it to keep the alignment high. We also undermine alignment when we block forward momentum instead of redirecting it.

Perfect Phrases to Redirect Efforts Without Stifling Creativity

If we or our developing leaders create alignment and get people on board by condemning misdirected efforts, we do it at the cost of energy. Dynamic Leaders embrace the forward momentum of misdirected creative innovation and redirect the action. These phrases point that momentum in directions that coordinate with existing obligations. (Note, as with all the phrases, only use them if you can state them sincerely. Otherwise you're manipulating.)

- Tell me again, in your own words, the target we are all aiming toward. Now, describe why this is the most important thing we can do to move in that direction.
- OK, but let's remember our target is ___________. How can we best move there?
- If you were a tennis player, I'd say your backswing was brilliant, but you need to adjust your aim to hit the right target.
- When someone presents something that is creative but not in alignment with goals, how do you like to tell them? I ask because I want to know how I can redirect your efforts without stifling your creativity.
- When you present something that is creative but not in alignment with goals, how do you like people to tell you? I ask because I hear some things in your words that might stifle the creativity of the people you're redirecting. I'd like for us to figure out how you can redirect them more creatively.

→ The creativity in this _______ (report, idea, etc.) is stimulating. Harness that creativity in the direction of __________ (target), and we'll move forward beautifully.

→ That wasn't what I had in mind. You display brilliant creative thinking here. If we clarify what we're going for without losing the momentum, nothing will stop us.

→ While I like it, I see it as off target for our _______ (goals, mission). Before I tell you why and how, I want you to consider where it might be off or convince me that it is on target.

→ It is brilliant. It just isn't what I pictured. Before I tell you, imagine what might be different between what you did and what I pictured from our talks. Then let's develop the same vision in the future.

→ Use the creativity you invested in this either to aim your efforts more in the direction of _______ (clarified target) or to convince me why this is on target with our _______ (goals, mission, objectives, values, etc.).

→ While your work is great, we must have failed to understand one another when we identified __________ as the target. Let's review where our communication went awry.

→ My first impulse when I discover work that is not in alignment with my goals is to point out what's wrong. I have to check myself and embrace the brilliance of the effort so I don't stifle creativity. I agree the activity you describe sounds off target. Let's figure out how you can point that out without being a total "buzz-kill."

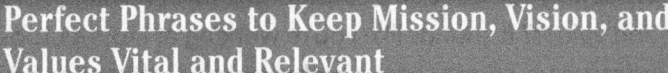

Perfect Phrases to Keep Mission, Vision, and Values Vital and Relevant

Mission, vision, and values stabilize purpose and direction when we express and observe them. If we ignore them, we miss a powerful alignment resource. Even when organizations don't have clear mission, vision, and values, these phrases create our own to access the power those tools bring to our leader development process. They also guide emerging leaders to take the initiative to keep mission, vision, and values alive and well in their spheres of influence.

- If we take the time to establish shared mission, vision, and values, we'll travel with the same map.
- Can you explain our organizational mission, vision, and values? What do they mean to you?
- Let's review our organizational mission, vision, and values and reflect on what they mean to us as well as how they apply in this particular case.
- We need to know what we're doing, what we seek to create here, and why we're doing it. We all apply values whether we know it or not, so let's figure out what we hold as important.
- It sounds like you're trying to influence people who have lost their connection to mission, vision, and values. How can you reignite those with them?
- What do you consider your main mission? Vision? Values?

- What do your associates consider the main mission, vision, and values? It sounds like you're working at cross-purposes because you don't share a higher vision. Let's look at how to address that.
- My mission in this process is ___________. I picture you/us ___________ (concrete depiction of outcome) in the next year/five years. I do this because I value ___________ (specific values).
- Let's put our ideas together to create our shared mission, vision, and values.
- Is it a value or a façade? If we don't support it in deed, it is a façade.
- I want us to cocreate mission, vision, and values because I value collaboration, reciprocal engagement, and synergy. If we develop these together, they'll be more relevant and dynamic.
- What changes would you make in our mission, vision, and values? Why?
- Mission, vision, and values change—not for convenience but because we grow from who we are when we set them. It's more of an evolution.
- Tell me what values you balanced when making that decision, and how each weighed in.
- Let's review our overarching values as well as how those values translate into day-to-day decisions.
- When we began, an overarching value was ___________ (e.g., to be open to possibilities). Now I say we've moved to where ___________ (e.g., developing specific skills) is of

higher value. I recommend that value guide our process now. Do you agree?

- I couldn't find a way to preserve both accuracy and expediency, so I favored expediency. Let's debrief on this and see what we can learn.
- What values are __________ (group or people our emerging leaders seek to guide) balancing here?

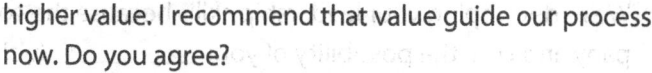

Perfect Phrases to Connect Emerging Leader Ideas to Mission and Values

Once we have our missions, visions, and values established, these phrases reinforce them by applying them to emerging leaders' innovations. They also guide emerging leaders to apply mission, vision, and values to the people they seek to influence.

- Let's test these ideas to see how consistent they are with our mission, vision, and values.
- How do you tie that idea in with our mission, vision, and values?
- I like that idea in terms of the values it represents. I'm a bit concerned that it doesn't reflect our leader development mission as well as it could. How could we adjust it to align with the mission?
- That's a very creative idea! If it passes our mission/vision/values test, I say we do it.
- If we're serious about __________ (leader development vision), we need to make sure everything we do supports that.

→ We're developing your leadership skills because the company and I see the possibility of your ________ (vision for emerging leader). I see your idea as ________ (on or off target) for that because ________.

→ I like that idea in terms of our leader development process for you. It would give you fantastic experience. I don't see how it supports our company mission of ________, however. How can we find an option that supports both objectives?

→ While that ________ (idea, decision, direction) may seem expedient in the short term, it is contrary to our values and is off the table.

→ Ask ________ (person in emerging leader's domain of influence) what values they considered in their decision. That will help enliven values and re-create alignment.

Perfect Phrases to Create Quick Idea Discernment Filters

These phrases create a predeveloped process for emerging leaders to apply to decisions. That process gives emerging leaders tools to be decisive with the confidence that results are aligned with the target.

→ How do you make decisions? What are the steps? What criteria do you use?

→ Bottom-line decision filter—is this something you're willing to be accountable for?

- A good discernment filter is like a good coffee filter. It removes the grinds without having to do it by hand.
- How do you know you have enough information to make a decision? Let's avoid paralysis by analysis.
- When I have a decision to make, here's what I do.
- How can our mission/vision/values help us make quick decisions?
- When you subject your decision to the mission, vision, and value criteria, what conclusion do you reach?
- Before I make a decision, I ask myself, ___________ (am I reacting or responding, what's the opportunity cost, what would the customer's experience of this be like, etc.)? Let's apply those questions to your decision.
- How would you adapt my filters to your decision-making process?
- What's missing from my criteria?
- Let's translate our mission, vision, and values into a specific list of criteria for you to apply when you're ready to make a decision.
- These filters empower you to be more autonomous and know your decisions complement rather than conflict with other efforts. Are you committed to applying them?
  - We'll review the criteria at our next meeting to see how they're working.
- It sounds like people are seeking approval from you for decisions they should be able to make themselves. How can you guide them and give them tools to be able to make those decisions without consulting you?

Perfect Phrases to Encourage Emerging Leaders to Present Ideas and Express Concerns

These phrases make it easy for emerging leaders to present their ideas, questions, and concerns and otherwise be heard. They swing the communication doors wide-open, which increases alignment. They also guide emerging leaders to make it easy for others to share ideas with them.

- Working together without trust is as disastrous in leading as it is in trapeze acts.
- Do you feel safe addressing issues and concerns with me?
- I like it when you challenge me. It shows you're engaged.
- I'm really excited about this idea, but don't let my excitement inhibit any questions or concerns you have.
- If you wonder whether to say something or not to say something, err on the side of overcommunicating instead of undercommunicating. If it gets overwhelming or feels intrusive, we'll work that out later.
- You're not here to please me or make me feel good about myself. You're here to learn, so let me know about anything that helps you develop—and me, too.
- They say the only stupid question is the one you don't ask. I believe it and want you to ask as many questions—stupid or otherwise—as you choose to.

- Please habitually ask three questions about anything I propose, even if you have to fake a few. You'll be surprised how many unasked questions that uncovers.
- Is there anything I do that inhibits you from asking me questions or expressing concerns and ideas?
- You can't lead without input and engagement. How can you make it safe for your associates to ask questions or express concerns and ideas to you?

Perfect Phrases to Foster Collaborative Thinking

There is wisdom in the saying, "two minds are better than one." These phrases encourage emerging leaders to collaborate with us and others and to create synergetic alignment. You'll find more useful phrases about problem solving in Chapter 9.

- I'm less concerned about who thinks of an idea and more concerned with how great the idea is.
- Collaboration is about individuals contributing ideas, experience, and expertise—and having fun doing it. I look forward to playing with possibilities!
- This is an exploration, not an argument.
- Instead of saying, "yes, but" to ideas, let's see if saying, "yes, and" can work instead. Even if the initial idea isn't wonderful, the "and" approach can lead to something spectacular.

- → Children playing together generate the most amazing ideas because they don't critique ideas and don't know what isn't possible. They just generate ideas and explore opportunities. I'd like us to keep that mind-set when we work together until we're ready to evaluate the ideas.
- → Let's see what our ideas spark in each other.
- → Two heads are better than one if they're working together.
- → I know we're used to thinking competitively and striving to be the one to come up with the best idea. I'd like us to move beyond that and let the idea matter more than who thought of it.
- → If you can get everyone thinking together on this issue, you're likely to come up with ideas none of you could have come up with on your own. Plus, you'll have buy-in.
- → It sounds like people are competing to have the best idea rather than thinking collaboratively. How can I help you to shift that?
- → How can you get everyone thinking as a team?

Perfect Phrases to Coordinate Innovation with Existing Obligations

Real crime scene lab investigators must laugh at the TV versions of their jobs, where there are specimens to analyze from two crimes per show/shift, most which turn out to be closely related. Real life isn't so tidy, and there are always other demands dividing our attention. Squeezing innovation into our agenda is a challenge. These phrases coordinate innovation with existing obligations.

- Let's consider that idea in relation to our/my/your/your associates' existing obligations.
- It's like we've been looking at how to redecorate, and now we're thinking about knocking out walls. Before we do that, let's make sure that's what we want. We'll need to identify and drop our "redecorating" plans if we take this direction.
- How do you balance innovation with existing obligations?
- At this stage in the project, is it beneficial to consider changing direction, or are we better off focusing our innovative thinking on how to execute our current direction better?
- How can we piggyback that activity with something we're already doing to make it efficient?
- Let's take a look at how we can do that without taking away from our ________ (sales, service, focus, etc.) in the area of ____________.

- Convince me that adopting your idea is more beneficial than meeting our existing commitments.
- Could someone else benefit from, or learn by, taking over any of our current obligations?
- Great idea! Let's weigh it with our existing obligations and see if the time is right or if we should park it until it is.
- You can't time innovation. It is always welcome. At this point, let's see how we can integrate it with other obligations.
- If we do this, you'll need to guide your associates about how to integrate the new initiative with their existing obligations. They'll need clear priorities.
- Let's create weekly objectives for the next month, monthly objectives for the next year, and yearly objectives for the next five years that tie these ideas in with existing obligations.
- They might think it's a great idea but have trouble figuring out how to implement it because of their existing obligations.

CHAPTER 6

Perfect Phrases for Developing Visionaries

A Dynamic Leader empowers others to develop and communicate clear visions of possibilities. A clear vision mobilizes energy for action. Going from being responsible for executing plans to being responsible for developing a vision is a challenging transition for emerging leaders. Previous chapters guided the Dynamic Leader to lead the process of developing a vision for the mentoring relationship and using visioning as an aspect of creating energy and increasing alignment. These phrases emphasize visioning itself as an essential Dynamic Leader ability.

Perfect Phrases to Get Emerging Leaders to Think Imaginatively

Moving from frontline roles into the leadership arena requires a shift in focus from "what tasks have to be done" to "what reality could be created." These phrases get leaders beyond thinking about "what is" to "what could be."

- → Let's imagine, create, and propose innovative solutions to ___________.
- → Imagination is a muscle—and we're building ours.
- → We need a creative solution here. What can you think of?
- → How do you prepare yourself to generate creative ideas? I'll tell you what I do when you finish.
- → How do you encourage creativity in others?
- → How do you see imagination playing a role in leadership?
- → What markets could you imagine us developing that we haven't yet?
- → What's the most imaginative thing you've ever done in a business setting?
- → Complete this sentence: Imagine a world where _____________. Be specific.
- → Complete this sentence: I'd be really surprised if we were able to ___________.What's the craziest idea you can think of about how to ___________?
- → In your wildest imagination, where could we (should we) be five to ten years from now?

- If you had unlimited resources, where would you take this company?
- Look for the patterns in the chaos in the marketplace. That's where our future is.
- What unique vision can we build on toward the future?
- What does your intuition tell you about this situation?
- Thinking boldly, what would truly excite you? That's a clue for building your vision.
    - What excites you about this idea?
    - What scares you about this idea?
- Do you see blocks to my creativity I don't?

Perfect Phrases to Develop a Clear, Comprehensive Vision

Imagination starts with random thoughts. A clear, comprehensive vision filters, organizes, and gives shape to haphazard imaginings. These phrases lead emerging leaders from unfocused dreams to a vision that is lucid and all-encompassing.

- Where do you envision yourself being at the end of this leadership development process?
- When you think about our firm, what do you picture in the future?
- What percentage of your time do you dedicate toward creating a long-term vision of the future? It's a leader's job to do that. I suggest you schedule more time for it.

- When you think about your own development, what do you envision?
- When you picture our organization in three to five years, what do you see?
- How can you describe your ideas to convey a compelling image of the future?
- Paint the picture of your vision so people see themselves in it.
- Write a science-fiction story that shows where this company (business, product line, you) can be ten years from now. How does this vision of the future connect to our organization's past and present?
  - Write an optimistic version and a pessimistic version.
  - What do these stories tell us to begin doing differently now?
- Why should we care about your vision?
- Why do you care about your vision?
- How does your vision serve the world?
- What assumptions does your vision make?
- How does your vision reflect the aspirations of people who have a hand in making it happen?
- Is your vision challenging, inspiring, clear, comprehensive, and specific?

Perfect Phrases to Encourage Emerging Leaders to Think Strategically

Leaders who imagine impractical possibilities and leave it to others to make them work are dreaming, not leading. By balancing imagination and practicality, these phrases foster strategic thinking.

- We need a plan for our visions. Otherwise we're dreaming.
- How do you define "strategic thinking"? Our strategy is our sustainable advantage.
- What differences do you see between visioning and strategizing? How are these terms related?
- We've envisioned what we want. How are we going to get there?
- What do we do next? What clear intermediate stages are there along the way?
- What ________ (financial, material, information, personnel) resources do we need to accomplish our vision?
- What do you plan to do first in your leader development process (or other objective)?
- What steps will you take to turn your ideas into reality?
- In broad terms, how would you create a plan for a leader development program (or other project)?
- Let's create weekly objectives for the next month, monthly objectives for the next year, and yearly objectives for the next five years.

- Let's walk through an analysis for that idea to evaluate the strengths, weaknesses, opportunities, and threats involved.
- Who are our allies for an initiative like this?
- Who might feel threatened by this initiative?
- Can we minimize the perceived threat? If we can't, is it worth risking? Why?
- Define the position of this idea in terms of market, environment, and measurement.
- What criteria do you use to find practical solutions to problems?
- How do you decide if an idea is practical or not?
- Who else should weigh in on this project?
- How could I think more strategically?

Perfect Phrases to Inspire Emerging Leaders to Think Globally

That idea that looks so good can have a strong negative impact on someone else or completely fall flat because of global events that escaped notice. These phrases remind us to think globally, outside the bounds of our own organizations.

- Describe this idea from a truly global perspective.
- List the countries where we (1) sell the product, (2) advertise the product (in the native languages and cultures),

(3) have sales and service offices, (4) engage suppliers, (5) have manufacturing sites, (6) face competitors, (7) integrate into the cultures, and (8) __________.

- What do you see as our market share rank in each of those countries?
- What does the new environment require now that it didn't before?
- How does social media (or other emerging technologies or trends) play into this initiative?
- This isn't the world it was where we can do things like this in secret. We need to make our choices assuming they are transparent.
- Can we develop this quickly enough to compete in this environment?
- What companies or people might this initiative impact?
- What departments or people in our company might this initiative impact?
- Have you validated this idea with ________ (representative of the target customer groups) from ________ (country)?
- If our chief competitor was looking at this initiative, what problems or opportunities might it find?
- What other companies have the capability of making this same product? Can they do it better, faster, or cheaper than we can?
- Is there a new technology on the horizon that might make our product obsolete soon?

- Are there regulatory agencies that might need to weigh in before we go too far?
- Have you monitored the news, press releases, and the social media to get the context for this?
- What's changed since we first considered this?

Perfect Phrases to Inspire Emerging Leaders to Embrace Input from Diverse Demographics

The workplace in the days of "Leave It to Beaver" was a homogeneous land of white, middle-aged men walking with firm steps. The new demographics are far more diverse. We all have some prejudices. The Dynamic Leader must harvest and channel diverse viewpoints and expectations into productive results. While this may involve a larger, organization-wide initiative, these phrases identify issues and solutions.

- I am committed to creating and sustaining an inclusive diverse workplace without bias. Please join me in this ongoing effort.
- When I started my career, the workplace was almost exclusively made up of white males. It's a different world now, and I still uncover unconscious assumptions and rankist attitudes in myself at times. When we observe those in each other, let's agree to point them out.
- I ask myself if there are people I work with who make me feel uncomfortable, and why. I'd like you to ask yourself the same questions.

- I ask myself if there are people I am not working with because they make me feel uncomfortable, and why I feel uncomfortable around them. I'd like you to ask yourself the same to make sure there is no implicit or explicit intolerance.
- What can we do to get comfortable with demographics we're not used to?
- Do we actually have a fully diverse workforce? If not, why not? How can we remedy that?
- What are we missing out on by not having every single employee fully engaged?
- Do you notice areas of unnecessary conflict and chaos that are due to ignoring the diversity of our workforce?
- What barriers might ________ (a specific new initiative) present to members of our diverse workforce?
- What areas of expertise or different perspectives might different employee experiences, cultures, viewpoints, and perspectives provide that we are now missing out on?
- What communication barriers do we experience due to different ages, races, genders, nationalities, or disabilities? How can we bridge them?
- Is it possible that some of our diverse employees don't feel comfortable providing input? How can we find out? What can we do to remedy that?
- Does my language and leadership approach demonstrate inclusiveness?
- May I give you some feedback on what your remark (suggestion, idea, etc.) suggests about your attitude toward inclusiveness?

Perfect Phrases to Share Your Personal Successes and Lessons

Sharing our leadership stories personalizes the leader visioning process. There is one caveat, however. Make sure you share your story for your emerging leader's benefit, instead of your own gratification. Make the communication specific to the emerging leader.

- Is there anything specific you would like to know about my experiences in leading?
- Before I could lead well I had to overcome my ______ (fear of, habit of, tendency to, beliefs that, etc.). I share this because ______.
- My first leadership experience was ______. I saw I was good at ______ (leadership skill). I also discovered I needed to develop ______ (another leadership skill).
- We all have our own roads to where we are, and I'd like to share mine in case it's useful to you.
- My thinking about leadership changed when I discovered ______.
- You'll get a kick out of this. One of my biggest leadership mistakes was when I ______.
- One of the best things I ever did as a leader was when I ______.
- The most influential leader in my life is/was ______.

- The most important thing in leadership in my experience is to ________.
- I was a leader for a long time before I thought about how I did it. I've had to reflect to be able to support your process. I realized ________. Thank you for causing me to do that.
- I wouldn't be in a leadership position if it weren't for ________.
- I learn a lot from reading about leadership. I applied one thing I read, ________ (specify), with ________ (results).
- I found ________ (sources) useful for leadership information.
- Let me tell a very brief story about when I faced a similar challenge in the past. This is what I did: ________. Can that help us here?

CHAPTER 7

Perfect Phrases to Develop Leadership Language

A Dynamic Leader both speaks and empowers others to speak as leaders. There's a saying that if it walks like a duck and talks like a duck, it probably is a duck. If you walk like a Dynamic Leader and talk like a Dynamic Leader, people regard you as a Dynamic Leader. And if you don't, they won't. May the walk precede the talk.

The phrases in this chapter develop language habits that demonstrate Dynamic Leadership. They empower our own words as we empower emerging leaders.

Perfect Phrases to Eradicate Victim Language

When we see ourselves as victims of circumstances, other people, lack of resources, or some other obstacle, it is impossible to move on and solve a problem. Sometimes our language reveals unconscious views even when we don't recognize our victimhood. When emerging leaders use victim language, these phrases call attention to the implications of their words and remind them that their own responses provide the greatest leverage they have in any situation.

- → You're talking like you have no power in this situation. Tell me what options you have.
- → The greatest leverage you have in any situation is your own response. How can you leverage it?
- → Are you playing a victim here? You always have choices, and you always have power. Your words sound like you don't. Let's explore options.
- → What are you going to do about that?
- → Who controls the story you tell? When you resist someone or something, they still define you. How can you make the story your own creation?
- → Let's stop talking about what's wrong with your team and start talking about what you can do as their leader to influence the situation.

- Let's stop talking about what we're going to try to do and talk instead about what we'll commit to. Name five options you have available.
- I'm open to reasons, but I'm hearing excuses for not moving forward. Let's look at how you can respond to the situation.
- You talk like this is something you *have* to do. It's not. It's something you *choose* to do as part of the larger objective.
- It doesn't matter how good you are if you discourage others.
- This isn't something that is happening to you. It's something that's happening with and around you. Let's look at the choices you're making and what other choices you have.
- I'm going to challenge you whenever you use the words *always, never, should, but,* and *have to*. Those are victim words.
- Words create reality. What kind of reality does your word choice invoke?

Perfect Phrases to Get Emerging Leaders to Translate Complaints into Requests

Dynamic Leaders focus on possibilities instead of limitations. Complaints focus on limits; requests focus on possibilities. These phrases discern between a complaint and a request.

- Are you here to complain or to make a request?
- How can we translate that complaint into an invitation or request?
- I hear a complaint as a whine that sounds weak. A request is a gracious expectation that sounds empowered. What do you want?
- You told them what you don't want. Have you clarified what you *do* want?
- Let's find the gem inside the grumble, the insight inside the insult, and the creative outlet for the complaint.
- Let's acknowledge negativity, and move to creative resolution and shared goals.
- To keep from sounding like a whiny complainer, let's shift our main focus from complaints to requests.
- I'm hearing about what you don't have and about the limits you face. I'd like to hear about what resources you do have, how you can use them, and how to move beyond limits.
- We're getting stuck in the problem. I want to hear you talk about solutions. What do you want?
- Let me tell you how I respond when you complain. A part of me wants to take care of you because you sound like

a helpless victim. Another part of me wants to shake you because I know you're not. I don't enjoy either response and invite you to gather your resources and tell me what you want or what you're going to do about the situation.

- Before you come to me with a problem, please consider solutions or ideas. I don't need you to have great answers before you come, just to have explored possibilities on your own.
- So what are you going to do about it?
- If I ever need a good swift kick to get me out of a whining mode, let me know.
- It sounds like you're dealing with victim language with your associates. Help them understand what that means, and give them an understanding of leadership language before you address the specific issue.

Perfect Phrases to Change Follower Language into Leadership Language

When emerging leaders speak like they're looking outside of themselves for answers and solutions, these phrases redirect their language from follower language into collaborative leadership language.

- I expect you to be a Dynamic Leader and to sound like a Dynamic Leader. You are not doing that now.
- What do you see as the difference between leader language and follower language?

- Are you the leader or the follower here? Are you acting the part?
- Are you speaking as the leader you need to be here?
- If you want to be thought of as a leader, focus less on what others say and tell me what *you* say.
- It's great that you're so well-read and listen to others. Now, instead of telling me what they say, talk to me from your own point of view.
- Have you developed your own point of view on this? That's the perspective I want to hear.
- I'll give you fodder for your own thoughts, but I'm not going to tell you what to think.
- I already know what I think. I want to know what you think. Decide and tell me clearly.
- If I want to know what ________ (other leader) thinks, I'd study him/her. I'm more interested in you and what you have to say.
- OK, so based on what ________ (other leader) thinks, what action do you recommend here?
- I'm interested in your own developed point of view and an explanation of how you reached it. I'm also interested in hearing you describe it in a way that sounds like you believe it, not that you're looking for me to validate it.
- Whose decision is this? Isn't the outcome your responsibility? Listen to their input, but decide for yourself.
- Leaders commit to specifics. Tell me what you just told me in on-the-ground specifics.

- Imagine ________ (some leader the emerging leader admires) was saying what you just did. How do you think he/she would say it?

Perfect Phrases to Change Commanding Language into Collaborative Leadership Language

Should our emerging leaders err on the side of rigidity and aggression, these phrases guide them back to more collaborative communication styles that invite input from others without abdication.

- I suggest you collaborate here.
- Be less commanding and more collaborative here.
- Your language is too commanding and that stifles contributions. Let's work toward a collaborative style.
- How would you define "collaborative leadership"?
- I often have trouble getting people to take a stand. Not you. I do find it's a challenge to get you to really consider other perspectives. How can we make that happen without losing the power of your commitment to your ideas?
- When you speak this way, I feel an impulse to oppose you out of principle or comply out of avoidance. What do you suppose it is about how you talk that feeds those desires?
- How does that kind of language work with ____________ (direct reports, clients, etc.)?

- When you ________ (action), how do others respond?
- A smiling tyrant is still a tyrant. I see you smile and monitor your vocal tone, but I'm hearing and feeling pressure and coercion in your words.
- Do you get a lot of input from others? If not, why do you think that is? Might you come across as bossy?
- There's a fine balance between coming across as indecisive and coming across too strong. I suggest you lighten your tone a bit.
- When you find yourself asking, "Why did you ____________?" take a step back and stand in the shoes of your listener. Are you putting that person through an interrogation?
- Sounds like you're pushing when you could be inspiring. How could you trade the stick for a carrot?
- How could you shift the tone of what you said from pushing to inspiring?
- Do you consider the others as your peers? I hear arrogance in your tone that suggests to me that you don't.
- Are there times I push instead of inspire?

Perfect Phrases to Encourage Showing Rather than Telling

Words that illustrate and paint pictures get results. These phrases encourage emerging leaders to use narratives to make points in ways that create vibrant, compelling images.

- OK, now show me rather than tell me.
- A picture is worth a thousand words, and a good story is worth a thousand pictures.
- Tell me a story about a story that changed you.
- You've told me facts. Now tell me a story. The best story always wins.
- What other stories could fit these facts?
- I'll tell you about a story I tell. It's been critical to my success.
- What stories have you told or do you tell that motivate others?
- While what you say makes sense, until you draw a picture, it never makes it into our hearts or imaginations.
- Analogies paint pictures and give a taste of experiences we haven't actually had. What analogy could you use to describe ___________?
- Please take each point and give me a concrete example of it I can relate to.
- Can you give me an example?
- I'm not picturing what you're talking about. Can you paint me a picture of it?
- Take your conversation with the team and tell it in story form from a team member's perspective.
- It sounds like your team members have a negative story running of ___________ (e.g., limitation, every person for themselves, etc.). What story would you prefer they tell? How can you create that picture convincingly for them?

- Are you reading your audience? It sounds like your story of ________ (e.g., redefining the industry, open communication, team power, etc.) isn't connecting. What story will inspire your listeners more?
- Tell me a story about the future of our organization.
- I've made a point to practice the kind of leadership I'm developing in you so you can experience it rather than just learn about it. How could you do that with your team?

Perfect Phrases to Encourage Inspiring Leader Language

Being right and knowing what you're talking about are not enough. These phrases inspire our emerging leaders to use compelling language to inspire and motivate others.

- Frankly, I'm bored by what I hear here and suspect others are too. Let's see if we can inspire ourselves and communicate that inspiration.
- Would you like some feedback on your language for your next meeting?
- When our meetings can't compete with text messaging, our wording needs more impact. Do we need to be more ________ (direct, active, vivid, succinct)?
- How can you express your idea so we see, touch, smell, and taste it?
- If your team members seem unmotivated, they need a better "why" with their what, when, and how.

- What symbols and metaphors can you create to describe your vision in inspiring terms that speak to hearts and minds?
- What is a good slogan for ___________ (initiative)?
- If this project had a bumper sticker, what would it say?
- Tell me your leadership philosophy in one crisp, clear message.
- Are you communicating in the right style for the audience?
- Let's use more dynamic language here. What words could we add to create sizzle?
- I heard a few words in your language that struck me as "buzz-kill." Want to know what they are?
- When I use words that kill the buzz you're feeling and block momentum, let me know. We'll both learn from rephrasing.
- How could you/I/we reword that to add sizzle and get people jumping out of their chairs to spring into action?
- One of the things I changed that has made my language more inspiring is ___________.
- What inspires you when you listen to a speaker? How can we apply that to how we talk?
- Do your actions inspire others to dream, learn, and act?

CHAPTER 8

Perfect Phrases to Handle Challenges

A Dynamic Leader sees problems and obstacles as invitations to outgrow the perspectives that created them and to embrace higher perspectives to transform them. These phrases prepare us to transform common challenges in the leadership development process into opportunities that take us and our emerging leader to the next level. They provide emerging leaders with the tools to handle challenges as, or even before, they arise.

Perfect Phrases to Overcome Reverse Delegation

We've all had emerging leaders hand us back projects they should handle on their own, or make requests for direction when they are capable of making the decision themselves. These phrases address that.

- Do you believe this is your problem to solve or mine?
- This is your problem to solve, not mine.
- I expect you to take the lead in solving this.
- What do you need to be able to carry this ball through to the end zone yourself?
- I threw you a ball here, not a boomerang. If your projects frequently come back to me, we need to consider how to change that.
- I could do this, but I trust you can take care of it. Ask me specific questions and I'll answer, after it's clear to me you've thought it through.
- I'll coach you through, but I won't do it for you. What do we need to review?
- What have you tried so far?
- What have you considered that you haven't tried?
- Which part of the project do we need to discuss to get the ball back in your court?
- What can I do to help you complete this on your own?
- What aspects of the project aren't clear? If you're having trouble completing this, I probably haven't been clear.

➜ I gave this to you because ______________, and I want to keep it in your court as much as possible. What can I do to support you doing this yourself?

➜ Would ______________ (training, consultation, resources, etc.) help you solve this?

➜ I'll help you when you're stuck, but I won't do it for you. I believe you can do this. Give it another try.

➜ This is a skill you need to master. I want you to have this learning experience. I'll invest the time for you to learn how to complete this project on your own.

➜ Is there any area where I've taken back control that I should let go?

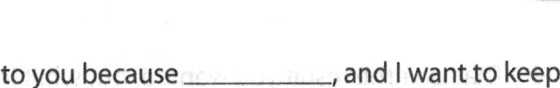

Perfect Phrases to Learn from Mistakes and Unsuccessful Efforts

These phrases help emerging leaders turn unsuccessful efforts into opportunities by exploring the thinking and understanding that lead to them. They use the lessons from failures to guide future efforts.

➜ Mistakes are inevitable, but I want you to learn from them to avoid repeating them.

➜ That isn't the result you wanted, but it shows you're stretching.

➜ That isn't the result you wanted, but what about it can we build on?

→ That isn't the result you wanted, but what lessons we can learn from it?

→ I do have a few questions about why you did it this way, and a whole list of things I learned from how you went about it.

→ I figure we just invested ________ (cost of mistake) in your development. I want to make sure we get our money's worth out of it in lessons learned.

→ Let's debrief what happened and see what you would have done differently, with the benefit of twenty-twenty hindsight. We're not back where we started—we're ahead of where we started because we know things we didn't before this happened.

→ Let's create a cause-effect diagram to identify all the causes that contributed to this problem. With these in hand, we'll decide what to do to keep this from happening again.

→ You're one *no* closer to a *yes*—one failure closer to a success.

→ Glad we got that mistake out of the way. How can we use it to move forward?

→ Because of ________ (mistake, impact, etc.), what have you learned, and how will you clean it up?

→ From a leadership point of view, that was a great endeavor. As your manager, I need to review it from a management point of view and talk about how we balance both.

Perfect Phrases to Hold Emerging Leaders Accountable

These phrases create accountability by eliciting and administering concrete and specific commitments. This is a management aspect of leadership development.

- Do you truly believe you are doing your best here?
- I expect you to take charge here. You haven't. (Point out specifics.)
- As a leader development coach, I admire your creative ideas. I need to put on my manager hat now and ask, exactly what are you committing to do and by when?
- Please be more specific in the deadlines and outcomes you are committing to.
- We have a lot of ideas of what we want to do, hope to do, and plan to do. Let's talk about what you are absolutely committed to doing.
- Let's agree on priorities and commit to complete work in that priority order.
- Accountability language says, "I will do 'x' by 'y' date at 'z' time." Please affirm your commitment with that kind of concreteness.
- Do you claim full ownership of this project?
- We committed to this development and that requires a high level of commitment from you. I need to count on you saying what you'll do and doing what you say. Are you committed to that?

- We're investing our time, resources, and future possibilities in you. We don't do that lightly. Your inattentiveness to ____________ (specific detail) makes me wonder if we're making a wise investment. How can you show me that we are?
- If this were a lower level program I might let ____________ (mistake) slide. It's not. I expect accountability. I expect you'll make mistakes, and I also expect you to show up when you do.
- Mistakes are a part of all growth, learning, and development. I'm not condemning you for making such a big one. But I do expect you to clean it up.
- I expect mistakes. When you make mistakes it tells me you're thinking, making decisions, and taking risks. I also expect you to do whatever you can to clean it up.

Perfect Phrases to Rein in an Unaligned Emerging Leader

If emerging leaders run amuck, these phrases rein them in without extinguishing their creative and imaginative fires.

- We're getting off track here. Let me reiterate—our goals for this session are ____________.
- Out-of-the-box thinking is good, but let's stay close enough to at least see the box!

- You might be way ahead of the curve here. I admire forward thinking. However, you're not leading if no one is aligned with you.
- We seem to have lost our alignment. How can we get back on the same page?
- Is there something we haven't been able to talk about that is undermining our relationship? You seem distant.
- Tell me how you see that suggestion (idea, comment, request, decision) supporting our mission.
- What is your understanding of our goals?
- The reason why we initiated this process with such care was to create a partnership that we're committed to. Your actions suggest to me that you're more committed to yourself rather than us. Why would I think that? Is it true?
- We're interested in developing and aligning your leadership skills with our organizational goals. I get the impression you're using this process to position yourself for your own interests, independent of our company mission and interests. Am I right? How can we get you realigned?
- I find your ____________ (specific behavior) disruptive. Do you intend to disrupt our work? If so, why?
- I like your independent spirit, but you seem like a bucking bronco. If we keep getting thrown, we can admire you, but we can't relate to you or continue to work with you. Why aren't you aligned with us? Is there a problem we can address?
- Do we need to reevaluate our mission (vision, values)?

Perfect Phrases to Inspire an Unenergized Emerging Leader

If we pay attention, we can tell when emerging leaders lose their inspiration and enthusiasm. Their work starts to have a more mechanical feel to it. We might end a conversation wondering why we're not energized like we once were. If we push, we will only alienate the emerging leader further. These phrases reignite energy in downtimes.

- → You sound in a slump. How can I help?
- → Where'd you go? You're here, but you're not really present. What can I do to help relight your fire?
- → I remember your enthusiasm when we began this journey. I can't seem to get your interest anymore. How would *you* energize someone who seems to have lost his or her sparkle?
- → Remember what I told you about this being a mythic journey where there would be an abyss or two? Have we found one?
- → You seem less enthusiastic than you were. Is it true? Why?
- → Have I done something to dampen your enthusiasm?
- → Has someone else done something to dampen your enthusiasm?
- → This part of the process is a bit like Wednesdays. The week isn't fresh and new anymore, and it isn't complete either. We don't have to figure out how to make it to Friday—Thursday will do.

- Let's revisit the vision we created for this process. Have we lost sight of where we are headed and why?
- When we're done with this process, I picture you in a position to ________. Does that thought inspire you?
- Let's review your progress. When we started, you were ________ (where); now, I'm delighted to say that you are ________ (here). What do we need to do to help you get to our final goal?
- Do we need to reshape this project to help you regain your enthusiasm?

Perfect Phrases to Shift and Expand Limited Mind-Sets

Often we lose our momentum as a result of being stuck in problems and being unable to see the bigger picture where the solution lives. When our emerging leaders are thinking too small and can't see the forest for the trees, these phrases open up broader perspectives.

- We're too narrowly focused. Let's drop back and see the big picture again.
- Leaders think in stereo. They see the small picture and the big picture simultaneously.
- When your thinking gets stuck, it could mean you're thinking too small.
- Let's run that idea past a short-term and a long-term filter.

- → What if I told you you're thinking small? What would expand your thinking?
- → Where am I thinking too small? How would the ______ (big boss, CEO, division leader) frame this problem?
- → As a leader, you're responsible for more than your own function. That means you need to engage across the organization.
- → Sometimes we're so focused on the problem we can't see the solution.
- → Let's stand back as if it's ten years from now and look at the situation from that perspective.
- → Let's step outside of our own identities here and pretend we're __________ (the top leadership expert in the country, the inventor of Six Sigma, Steve Jobs, etc.) looking at what we're doing. What do you think he/she might suggest?
- → If anything were possible, what would you consider that you aren't now? We can talk about how to cut the pie, but let's see if we can make the pie larger instead.
- → In a perfect world with infinite resources, what would this project look like? How much of that could we actually accomplish?

Perfect Phrases to Address Follow-Through Issues

These phrases identify follow-through issues and problems in order to bring about solutions.

- When we establish agreements, I expect you to follow up on them.
- When you make an agreement, I find myself unsure of whether you will deliver or not. That is not acceptable for a developing leader.
- You agreed to ___________, not ___________ (what was done instead). I need to be able to count on your word.
- Let me slip out of a leader role now and embrace a manager role. I am concerned about our follow-through here (give specifics). How can we improve our follow-through?
- Are there resources you need? How can you get them?
- Dynamic Leaders say what they'll do and do what they say. That's not happening here. If you can't honor your commitments, don't make them.
- Are you having problems with someone reporting to you? Can you identify and solve those problems? If their follow-through affects yours, it's your issue to resolve.
- Is it possible that issues have come up that make it inadvisable to complete this project? What are they and why? What other direction should we turn instead?

- What organizational tools are you using? Are they satisfactory, or do you need something else?
- Is something blocking you from following up?
- Is this project still a priority for you? What other activities are competing for your time and attention?
- Why are there so many loose ends?
- How's my follow-through? Is there something that I have dropped the ball on?

CHAPTER 9

Perfect Phrases for Developing Change Champions

A Dynamic Leader empowers others to initiate needed changes. Today's market requires leaders at all levels who continually adapt, change, and update goals and processes. These phrases encourage and equip emerging leaders to move beyond their limitations and to initiate change in their own areas of influence and champion change on a broader scale. They also help employees influence others to embrace broader organizational changes as they are implemented.

Perfect Phrases to Inspire Emerging Leaders to Increase Autonomy to Make Change

These phrases guide emerging leaders to take their level of autonomy to the next level by testing and expanding limits.

- I want you to take more initiative here. Be bolder. (Give specific examples of missed opportunities.)
- Keep on walking (moving forward) until someone tells you to stop.
- Never be deliberately disrespectful, but if no one ever tells you you've exceeded your limits, you're playing it too safe.
- Imagine you are playing tennis. Aim for placing the ball right on the edge of the line.
- There are limits to what we can do. There are boxes we operate in. But they're often not nearly as narrow as we imagine. If we don't push against the walls, we'll never find out where they actually are.
- Take a look at the things you're getting approval for. Ask how many you could take independent action on. Then try it.
- If you need to call an audible, I've got your back.
- If you can't get the senior levels to push it through, what can you do at your own level? Once you've proven your idea, it will be easier to sell.
- Is it better to ask for forgiveness than permission here?
- Where do you see me asking for permission when I shouldn't?

Perfect Phrases to Encourage Innovation

These phrases encourage innovative ideas, projects, and processes.

- We need more innovation here. What ideas do you have?
- The way you ________ (action) is innovative. Innovation creates opportunity. Keep at it!
- I have some ideas of how we could approach this, but I prefer to hear yours first.
- What project was your personal best? Who initiated it?
  - Let's keep creating those kinds of opportunities. (If their personal best project was self-initiated.)
  - You can see what a difference that project made for you. Let's see how we can create those kinds of opportunities for yourself and others. (If the project was other-initiated.)
- If we couldn't keep doing ________ (project, procedure, task) the way we've been doing it, what would you recommend we do?
- Clearly our way of ________ (system) isn't working. What can we do that would work?
- What are we doing that we should stop? How can we?
- Where should I be innovative and I'm not?

Perfect Phrases to Encourage Challenging the Status Quo

Each organization has its own cultural trance. There are ways things are done, and anyone who questions the status quo is suspect. Dynamic Leaders encourage challenges to the status quo where everyone wins rather than where there are personal victories. When we encourage our protégées to challenge the status quo, the "enemy" is outdated goals and methods—not the people who champion them. These phrases arm the emerging leader to challenge the status quo.

- → Our old ways of working are not providing the results we need here. Please help us abandon unnecessary constraints and obsolete habits and find a better way.
- → I'm looking for revolution, not evolution. There must be a better way. Let's find it.
- → A diplomat avoids unnecessary conflict. A leader doesn't seek it out but does challenge group norms and rock the boat when necessary.
- → Every perception that constrains us is open to challenge.
- → If I or someone else resists a necessary change, challenge that resistance.
- → Who besides me do you have in your life who challenges your assumptions and practices? If you don't have anyone, find someone. Adapt and use his or her methods with others and with me.
- → Would you challenge my expectations to act consistently with your own values?

- Complete this sentence: Why can't people just wake up and start ___________?
- Complete this sentence: If I wasn't concerned about a reaction, I'd recommend an initiative to ___________.
- Complete this sentence: Why are we still ___________?
- Conventional wisdom isn't necessarily wise. It can lead to losses. Question and challenge it.
- Next time you find yourself justifying an action based on precedent, question whether you are championing the status quo instead of championing the best option.
- Is there new technology that we could use instead of doing things the same old way?
- Do you see a boat I need to rock?
- How do I preserve an outdated status quo?
- Are you encouraging your people to challenge how you do things? Or are you sending some kind of signal that tells them not to?

Perfect Phrases to Motivate Taking Charge

Dynamic Leaders do whatever it takes and look for others who do. They are willing and able to take charge and persevere. These phrases prompt and reinforce those qualities.

- Thanks for taking charge and ___________ (calling, handling some task, filling some need, etc.). That's exactly the kind of initiative we're building here.

- Taking charge doesn't require taking over. It can simply be picking up a dropped ball and putting it back into play.
- Where are you waiting for someone else to take action where you could take charge yourself?
- I expect you to take charge here. You haven't. (Point out specifics.)
- Identify areas that need work (things done, decisions made, issues resolved, loose ends). Then get them done.
- Where should you take the initiative?
- Taking charge in a leadership vacuum is taking charge of your destiny.
- If this were management development, you might wait for me to get the ball rolling. Since it's leadership development, the ball is in your court. Where do you want it to go?
- Take the leadership role in your own leadership development process. That way you'll get twice the benefit.
- Tell me about initiatives you've undertaken to improve procedures.
- Take charge of your learning here with me.
- Make a list of complaints you have. We'll turn it into a list of leadership opportunities for you to take charge of. That won't just develop your skills, it will move your own operations forward.
- I could lay out a plan for your development. I have lots of ideas. But you'll get the most out of this if you take the lead in making this work for you.
- I'd like to hear your ideas first and how you want to proceed. Then we can talk about mine.

- Find leadership opportunities and new ways to take charge everywhere. Start that process here, now, with you and me, in our relationship.
- If you were in charge of your own leader development, what would you do? You are in charge, so go for it.
- What do you want or need for me to do that I haven't done?
- What do you want to have happen? How can you make that happen?
- Where do you see me waiting for someone else to take action instead of taking charge?
- Where are you waiting for someone else to take action instead of taking charge? Why?

Perfect Phrases to Encourage Emerging Leaders to Move Out of Their Comfort Zones

These phrases guide emergent leaders beyond their comfort zones and keep them fully aware while they operate there.

- I want you to have the courage to do the right things here, even if they are unfamiliar, uncomfortable, and difficult.
- We are moving into a new area now. Inevitably it will be uncomfortable for you. We need to work through that discomfort to a new level of operating.
- If you're feeling awkward and uncomfortable, it shows you're trying something new.

- ➜ Stepping outside your comfort zone is amazing—it makes the zone bigger.
- ➜ It's hard to stay fully connected to your resources and resilience while you cling to your comfort zone. Remind yourself that you always have choices.
- ➜ Whose comfort zone are you controlled by?
- ➜ Do you have control of your comfort zone, or does your comfort zone control you?
- ➜ Facing discomfort is a key ingredient to expanding your comfort zone.
- ➜ Comfort isn't a decisive criterion for action. If an initiative creates a lot of discomfort in you, we'll examine it for practicality to see if your discomfort is a warning signal. Otherwise, I consider it a leader development opportunity signal.
- ➜ I don't expect you to be comfortable as you step into new activities. I just expect you to stay conscious, alert, and resourceful.
- ➜ What tools do you have to help you work effectively despite discomfort? What do you need? How can you get them?
- ➜ What comfort zones do you see me staying in? How can you help me expand?
- ➜ How do you help people walk through situations that take them out of their comfort zone?

Perfect Phrases to Help Emerging Leaders Transcend Oppositional Thinking and False Choices

What is oppositional thinking? It's black and white, either/or, right or wrong thinking that favors one side of life's polarities in opposition to the other. Conflicting values and paradoxes are facts of life. Speed often does come at the cost of quality. Teamwork can diminish individual initiative. Oppositional thinking regards these contrasts as either/or choices without considering how the opposites can actually complement or at least balance each other. In his book *The Crack Up,* author F. Scott Fitzgerald said, "The test of a first-rate intelligence is the ability to hold two opposing ideas in the mind at the same time and still retain the ability to function."

These phrases redirect emerging leader oppositional thinking into confluent conscious choices that find the best blend of qualities.

- Is this a false dichotomy? Do we really need to choose one option or the other?
- How can we integrate options or find a balance between them or move in some new direction that provides all we need?
- I believe we've fallen into accepting a false dichotomy here. Let's reject that fallacy.
- We can talk about how to cut the pie, but let's see how we can make the pie larger instead.

- Are these really opposing alternatives, or might we find a way to combine these ideas?
- Our leadership and our management roles seem to be at odds. I'd like us to separate out the elements and see how they can be integrated.
- These ideas seem opposed. How can we combine them to create an idea that's better than either of them?
- These ideas seem opposed, but I think we can find their confluence.
- I'll bet a bit of creativity can uncover a blend of these competing strategies that will surpass the promise of each.
  We're blinded by a false dichotomy here. Let's reject the false choice and create new alternatives.
- We may need to sacrifice some ________ (e.g., speed) to accomplish ________ (e.g., quality), but I'm not ready to make that decision yet. Let's keep going to see how we can achieve both.
- You can offer a different opinion without negating the first one.
- Instead of starting our response with "yes, but," let's begin it with "yes, and." We may need to drop aspects of this idea, but let's see if we can build on it, not tear it down.
- Instead of a different perspective, offer an expanded one.
- It would be easier to choose between these options, but ultimately if we can find a way to embrace the whole, we'll have a much better outcome.

- Let's go for ____________ (e.g., sales *and* profit, vision *and* execution). If we make a choice between them, let's be sure we know why.
- Almost every situation has a solution where everyone wins. We need to continue to explore creative alternatives until we all get a yes.
- Instead of saying "this *or* that," let's try "this *and* that" and see where we go.

Perfect Phrases to Inspire Confluent Debate

In a table tennis game, your opponent is also your partner. You play in opposition to win, but there is an underlying confluence of intention. You "have at" each other to enjoy a good game. Confluent debate is like a table tennis game where the oppositional nature of how you play is based on an underlying shared intention of reaching the best conclusion.

The word *debate* has its roots in the word *debatre*, "to fight, to contend, to beat down." While debate is defined as arguing and disputing, it also is defined as discussing and considering. Dynamic Leaders will fight, argue, and dispute, but they do it for clarity, not to overpower. When Dynamic Leaders discuss and consider ideas, they are also willing to challenge them. Although the word *debate* does not refer to the quality of confluence, other words have their limits as well. For example, the common use of the word *dialogue* is too neutral for our purposes. *Debate* is used here despite its imperfection.

The phrases here invite emerging leaders to "confluent debate" in the sense of forming and voicing their independent points of view. They invite emerging leaders to test their own perspectives in relation to contrasting perspectives and to challenge contrasting perspectives in relation to their own. Some even suggest the emerging leader try on black-and-white perspectives to generate ideas. The goal of this confluent debate is a more comprehensive perspective that meets all challenges.

- ➜ Spar with me on this. It will get the ideas and energy flowing.
- ➜ Play devil's advocate here for me.
- ➜ Pretending you are our main competitor and this project could put you out of business, tell me why this project business will fail. Tell me so convincingly that I tell you to drop it.
- ➜ Pretend you are our main competitor, and you want us to take this project on because you know it will clearly fail. Now convince me that this project will succeed.
- ➜ Let's argue this from a manager point of view and a leadership point of view as if they conflict. Then we can see how to integrate the two.
- ➜ Let's get black and white for now. Pretend there is only one side to this story—that this solution isn't going to work. What are your arguments?
- ➜ Tell me a story from the future looking back on this project. It's a sad story about what we missed in the beginning that caused the project to fail.

- Pretend you're our worst critic. What would you say to me?
- What assumptions are we implicitly making here? Are they valid? Can we challenge them?
- Now that you've shot down this idea, argue why it's a perfect one.
- Tell me what your gut is telling you.
- Are there any factors that I have overlooked or ideas I've quashed prematurely?

Perfect Phrases to Get Emerging Leaders to Make Their Ideas Practical

Some misguided leaders come up with big, vague ideas and consider implementation details as beneath them, or below their pay grades. These phrases make emerging leaders' ideas practical.

- That's an intriguing idea. Now we need an action plan to see just how practical it is.
- Leadership and management go hand in hand. That's a good idea, but in order for it to be a great idea, it needs to be manageable.
- I distinguish between dreams, notions, aspirations, goals, plans, and action items. All are useful, but for now I would like to move some of these concepts toward implementation.

- What idea should we begin with, and how can we make it specific and actionable? It's time to put feet on your ideas and see which ones can actually run a race.
- Let's put our management hats on for a moment. What would it take to make that happen? Do we have those resources now? If not, can we reasonably expect to get them in time?
- Is there a person or company we could partner with to make this happen?
- I asked you to imagine what we should do if we couldn't fail. Now that we have that list, let's ask the next questions: How likely is the success of these ideas? How can we make them practical?
- What steps do you recommend for a strategic analysis of this idea?
- Let's look at whether the ideas really reflect reality.
- Which of these ideas are ahead of their times? Which ones can we develop and act on now?
- It's time for risk/reward and cost/benefit analyses of these ideas.

CHAPTER 10

Perfect Phrases to Develop Problem Solvers

Dynamic Leaders don't just help emerging leaders solve problems; they guide them to the next leadership level of exploring opportunities that problems contain. Every curveball is seen as a challenge to grow, develop, and expand. They are examined to see if they actually pave the way to a new objective that surpasses the original. The problem-solving process starts with taking ownership of problems and progresses into a highly creative and dynamic process.

Perfect Phrases to Get Emerging Leaders to Take Ownership of Problems

Taking ownership of problems is an essential first step of solving them. Taking ownership means committing to do whatever it takes to resolve the issue.

- → I want you to own this problem now, regardless of where it originated or who or what is to blame.
- → Owning a problem is like getting the deed to a run-down property. You may not have created the problem, but you own it and you're committed to solving it now.
- → We can't blame the "idiots in leadership" for what goes wrong any longer. We're them.
- → Taking ownership of this problem means paying a price should you fail to look after it—but getting the rewards when you solve it.
- → Is this something you're willing to be accountable for?
- → This is your problem. I'm not saying you created it. I'm saying how it is solved reflects on you.
- → You own the task of cleaning up this problem. Do you accept that ownership?
- → I see your ownership of this problem extending as far as ____________ but not including ____________ (e.g., getting the product ready for market but not contacting vendors). How do you see it?

- → How invested are you in solving this? I see this problem as a huge opportunity for your development—if you take ownership of it.
- → To give you a personal stake in solving this, I'm planning to ____________ (e.g., announce the positive results at a meeting, name the initiative after the emerging leader, etc.).
- → What would make you really be willing to own this problem?
- → Do you see any problems that I need to take ownership for that I haven't?

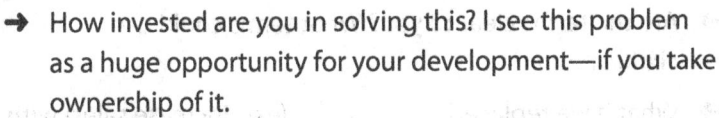

Perfect Phrases to Understand a Problem

These phrases define the problem so that the right problem can be solved.

- → Please state the problem you believe we must solve first.
- → Is there some related problem we should solve first?
- → Let's define the problem clearly before we try to solve it.
- → Restate the problem in your own words.
- → How can we rephrase that?
- → What's the real problem? What prior problem caused this problem? What prior problem caused that problem?
- → Can we circumvent or delay the process? Should we even take it on?

- Are the terms clear to you? What terms could use clarification?
- What if we replaced ____________ (e.g., increase sales) with ____________ (e.g., attract sales)?
- What's the opportunity in the problem?
- Let's stand back and look at it from a more general perspective.
- Would ____________ (another stakeholder) define the problem differently? What would he/she say?
- Let's rephrase the problem in positive words.
- Who should be involved in this process?
- What additional information do we need?
- Who else can help?
- Who is also affected by this problem?
- What is the worst that can happen if we don't solve it?
- What is the best outcome we can have if we do solve it?
- What am I not understanding about this problem?

Perfect Phrases to Inspire Emerging Leaders to Translate Problems into Possibilities

In Chapter 7, we guide our emerging leaders to translate complaints into requests. Here we guide them to shift the focus from problems to their solutions. These phrases use problems to create forward dynamic momentum instead of acting as barriers.

- We are facing an important and difficult problem here. We need to work together to solve it.
- I'm optimistic we can think creatively about solutions and gain essential insights.
- I find that often problems really are opportunities in disguise. It's not just a new age slogan or gobbledygook. It's true.
- Please think both practically and creatively, long term and short term. Everything is on the table, at least for now.
- We can see the problems as boulders or as stepping-stones. I say we look at them as stepping-stones.
- Do you see possibilities in this problem? Is it an opportunity in disguise?
- How could we turn this into a possibility instead of a problem?
- Who else faced this problem? How did they solve it?
- How can this problem benefit us?
- Every problem has a solution. If we focus on possibilities we are more likely to find them.
- If we tell ourselves it's going to be hard, it will be.
- Let's focus out the front window at what's ahead and only glance in the rearview mirror when we need to.
- We need to move to a new level of thinking from the one that caused the problem.
- Problems are a signal there's something for us to learn.
- Yep. That's a problem all right. What possibilities do you see in it?

- ➜ Tell me a story five years into the future where you look back at these seemingly insurmountable problems. Tell me how you resolved them.
- ➜ If I ever seem stuck on the problem, I invite you to help us move forward by focusing on the solution.

Perfect Phrases for Problem-Solving Brainstorming

Many of us have a difficult time suspending judgment during brainstorming. Premature evaluation stifles the creative brainstorming process. These phrases "dynamize" the brainstorming process.

- ➜ It is time to brainstorm for new ideas and approaches. Here is how I want to structure it.
- ➜ Let's think of possible solutions and keep going until we come up with twenty ideas. They don't need to be good ideas, but let's come up with twenty.
- ➜ A bad idea can lead to a good idea, so let's collect ideas and evaluate them later.
- ➜ Let's ask three who questions, three what questions, three when questions, three why questions, and three how questions.
- ➜ What are we trying to accomplish?
- ➜ How might we ________ (action) to ________ (result)?
- ➜ If we tried to make the problem worse instead of better, how would we go about it? What can we learn from that?

- Have we done this sort of thing before? How?
- Who can be asked to help here? Who has experience solving similar problems? How has that person done this?
- How could we increase (decrease) the scope (scale)?
- Where can we make substitutions?
- What if we changed the time line?
- Could we combine this with someone (something)?
- What if we did the opposite?
- What would happen if we didn't do anything at all?
- Is there anything I am doing that stops the brainstorming process?

Perfect Phrases to Evaluate Solutions

Once the list of possibilities is created, use these phrases to identify the most promising ideas.

- Let's look at our options and make a decision to move us forward.
- What value criteria will we use to identify the better ideas from this list?
- How does each possibility score against these ideas?
- What options are still standing?
- What would happen if we didn't do anything at all?
- Starting with the first idea, what are some pros? Cons?
- Let's vote to pick our favorite three ideas.

- Let's arrange our good ideas into a structure, such as a tree, hierarchy, or dependency diagram, to identify missing pieces.
- What ideas can we spin off of these ideas?
- What tools and resources would we need to implement this solution?
- What tools and resources do we need to solve that problem?
- Are there people or companies we could partner with to get the resources we don't currently have?
- How can we move to a simpler yet more effective solution?
- What criteria can we use to quickly eliminate some of these options (e.g., are there safety, legal, or regulatory issues with the proposed solution)?
- Can we economically outsource any components of our solution?
- What new problems can this solution create?
- What are the likely immediate and long-term consequences or advantages of each option?
- What problems might each of these options create?
- What additional information do you need to decide? Why is it crucial?
- Do you really need additional information or are you stalling a decision?
- Which options are the most desirable and the least desirable, and why?

- What is your final choice?
- Where will you start?

Perfect Phrases to Develop Resourcefulness

When we develop leaders, we offer ourselves as resources. But we don't want to be their only resources. These phrases help developing leaders draw from both outside and internal resources.

- I want you to think broadly about drawing on resources. What people, information, equipment, expertise, or other resources outside the organization could help here? What resources inside the organization could help?
- There's a saying that knowing where to look for the answers is as important as having the answers. Where can you go for the answers?
- Have we broadly considered where else we can go for help here? What other experts, resources, opinions, suppliers, or innovators can we tap?
- A researcher wouldn't write a research paper with only one book as a reference source. He'd have a whole library at his fingertips. How can we add to your resources?
- What tools can I offer you to solve this problem?
- When have you solved a problem like this before? What resources did you use?

- Think about everyone in your network who might be a resource to solve this problem that you haven't considered yet. Whom can you think of?
- Who wrote the book about this situation? Why not call him/her?
- Have you posted about this situation on your social networks?
- How do we get people to find a common approach to a problem?
- Whom do you regard as the absolute expert in this area? How can you learn from him/her?
- What resources might the team have that we haven't tapped into?
- Have I been an effective resource here? If not, where have I fallen short?

CHAPTER 11

Perfect Phrases to Develop Decisiveness

A Dynamic Leader guides emerging leaders to speak decisively. Decisiveness without problem solving is recklessness. When emerging leaders develop appropriate decisiveness, they make and implement choices based on a clear understanding of reality. Dynamic Leaders integrate and balance the qualities of decisiveness and careful analysis.

When the stakes are relatively low or the problem-solving process distills options into obvious choices, it doesn't take a lot of decisiveness to move forward. When the stakes are high or the best choices are not obvious, indecision can keep us paralyzed. These phrases develop decisiveness.

Perfect Phrases to Define Decisiveness and Identify Barriers to Decisiveness

Some people act with far too little data or input and are decisive to a fault. They see a diving board and jump right off, blithely assuming there is water in the pool. Other people couldn't make the decision to leave a burning building without a little more information first. We all have our own barriers to decisiveness. These phrases move the emerging leader forward by getting barriers on the table.

- Leaders are like knives in that they need to stay sharp and make clean and careful cuts.
- What do you see as the role of decisiveness in leadership?
- Do you have any disdain or concerns about the quality of decisiveness?
- Share a story about a time when you failed to take decisive action.
    - What kept you from acting?
    - What would have enabled you to act?
    - Were you afraid? What of?
    - What caused a lack of courage?
- Do you trust your own rational judgment?
- I know that I need to watch out for my own decisiveness when ____________. How about you?
- Have you ever failed to make a timely decision? What happened?
- How would you rate your decisiveness level?

- → What fuels your indecision?
- → How do you know you have enough information to decide?
- → Complete this sentence: I find it easy to be decisive when ___________.
- → Complete this sentence: I find it difficult to be decisive when ___________.
- → Tell me about a decision you made that proved ill-advised in hindsight. What was the result? How did you grow from it? How did it help make you the person you are today?
- → How could we summarize your barriers to decisive action?
- → How do you support decisive action among your associates?

Perfect Phrases to Overcome Barriers to Decisiveness

These phrases address the barriers to being decisive and create forward momentum.

- → Let's review a previous decision and learn from it.
  - → What would you do in that situation now?
  - → What resources do you have now that you didn't have then?
  - → What did you learn from this decision?
  - → What would you do differently today?
  - → Would a different (stronger) decision have made a difference? What would have that outcome been?

- What qualities do we need to develop to build decisiveness?
- How can we build on those qualities?
- Like other skills, decision making improves with practice. Don't think of this as a pass-fail test. Think of it as practice—and decide.
- What low-risk decisions can we start with and build up to bigger ones? This builds your decisiveness muscle.
- Every decision creates future problems. Failing to make a decision also creates problems. Either way, I have confidence in your ability to solve them.
- Here's a story about when I lacked decisiveness and what I learned from it.
- Here's a story about when I made a hasty decision and what I learned from it.
- What was the best difficult decision you ever made? How did you reach that decision? What powered your ability to be decisive in that situation?
- Are you afraid of making a wrong decision? There isn't such a thing. There are better and worse decisions, but not wrong ones.

Perfect Phrases to Challenge Indecisiveness When We Observe It

If we observe our emerging leaders waffling when they have what they need to decide, these phrases move them forward.

- It is now time to decide. Let's do it.
- Let's not overthink this. It's time to move forward and decide.
- You sound indecisive. Are you? Why?
- Let's not analyze this to death. You're ready to make the decisions.
- Isn't this your decision to make?
- Your commitment sounds halfhearted. Why is that?
- It sounds like you're hedging.
- Decide to act, decide not to act, or decide what you need to decide. Either get off the fence or figure out when and how you will.
- There comes a time to fish or cut bait. I think we're there, and it's time to give this our all or not do it.
- Your choice of the word *try* (or other noncommittal word) sounds indecisive. Are you, or is it just your wording?
- If you're going to lead, now is the time to lead.
- It strikes me that you have all the information you need to decide now. Why are you hesitating?

- If ________ (some leader the protégée respects) spoke that way, would you think he/she was being decisive?
- You sound unsure. Do you need more information or more decisiveness?
- In or out. In between gets you nowhere.
- Are you as indecisive as you sound?
- Decide now, decide not to decide, or decide when you'll decide. Not deciding is a decision. You can't avoid making a decision.
- If you had to decide right now, what would you choose?
- We've moved into the "just do it" stage. So tell me, just do what?
- If you're waiting for a perfect option to move forward, that won't happen. Decide.
- Increasing information has diminishing value after a point. Unless you can identify something specific and readily and quickly available that you need, I say decide.
- You can't know if your decision is right or wrong until you make it. If you wait too long, you'll miss opportunities and lose control of the decision-making process.
- How can I lead more decisively?

Perfect Phrases to Motivate Emerging Leaders to Be More Decisive

These phrases personalize the impact of decisive action and of indecision to motivate decisiveness.

- Becoming a more effective decision maker improves your career performance, increases your self-confidence, and demonstrates your leadership skill.
- I want you to be more decisive because I see the potential for ___________.
- You didn't get where you are by being indecisive. Tell me about a time you were effectively decisive.
- We practice decisiveness on the small stuff so when the big stuff happens, you have the skills and the habit to decide quickly and well.
- I've heard the hottest place in hell is for people who stay neutral when the situation calls for decisiveness. Neutrality can become a habit, and it's a hard habit to break when the stakes are high.
- Whom do you admire for his or her decisiveness? Tell me about decisions that person made. What did you admire about those decisions?
- Here's the best bad example of indecision I know. (Share story.)
- When I stopped agonizing over every decision, it set me free.
- Decisiveness makes you the author of your own destiny. You may not like every aspect of the story, but it's your story.

Perfect Phrases to Guide Decisive Action

While decisiveness is good, Dynamic Leaders avoid premature authoritarian decision making. Shooting first and looking second is not decisiveness. If an emerging leader seems trigger-happy, these phrases redirect him or her to make proper considerations before deciding.

- I'm afraid you're making a rash decision here. Please gather information representing broader perspectives and generate more alternatives before deciding.
- You're missing an opportunity here. Look deeply into the situation and then decide.
- Whoa! You are getting ahead of yourself here.
- I know a lot of people who agonize over decisions. It's refreshing to work with someone who doesn't do that. You, however, err in the other direction.
- "Ready, fire, aim" doesn't work well in the business world. It seems to me that's what you're doing here. It's important to understand the problem before we attempt to solve it.
- You just skipped a couple of steps in the decision-making process.
- I just witnessed the preemptive dismissal of a plethora of viable possibilities.
- This goes beyond decisiveness to "dismissiveness."
- This decision is premature. Consider more alternatives before you decide.

- Ensure you talk to (listen to, study, consider) ________, and give me a list of at least three viable alternatives before making this decision. Until you can describe a substantial list of alternatives and their pros and cons in depth you are not ready to make this decision.
- You must be able to represent all significant views fairly, proportionately, and without bias before deciding.
- This is too big of a decision to make impulsively. Let's revisit the decision-making process step-by-step.
- You seem in a hurry to decide quickly rather than take your time to really understand the situation. Is there an issue here?
- It sounds like some of your associates decide before they've really explored options. What can you say to them to get them to consider options first?

CHAPTER 12

Perfect Phrases to Recognize Success

We all like to be acknowledged when we accomplish something. It motivates us and inspires us to greater heights. These phrases recognize smaller and major successes, applauding advancements as well as accomplishments.

Being specific is a key to successfully recognizing success. General acknowledgments can seem like flattery. Specific acknowledgments demonstrate that we are, in fact, paying attention.

In the process of finding the words to adapt your recognition to a specific employee's efforts, you often discover things to acknowledge that would otherwise have been missed.

Perfect Phrases to Acknowledge Leadership Initiative

When a developing leader takes the initiative, these phrases acknowledge the quality of innovation and creativity. The outcome is secondary to the process in these phrases.

- I thank you for ___________.
- A leader's first job is to define reality. That takes initiative, and that's what you did. Thanks!
- Great initiative! What pleases you most about how it unfolded?
- It started as your vision, and now it's a shared one. Thanks!
- You knew the status quo wasn't working, and you created a new one that did. Thanks!
- It's never easy to wake a culture from its trance, but that's what you did. Thanks!
- No one ever thought to do this before. You not only thought of it, but you led the way and made it happen.
- You weren't just improving on reality here. You created a new reality. That took initiative.
- This was your idea. I'm making sure everyone knows that.
- What impresses me most was how you took the initiative to ___________.
- I want to sing your praises from the rooftops. How would you like for me to spread the news of how you went about this?

- May I go public and tell ________ (the board, CEO, etc.) about what you did here?
- You saw where you wanted to go, you got up, and you went there, taking the team with you. Way to go!
- That may not have been the result you wanted, but it shows initiative.
- You saw a difficult problem and took the initiative to address it.

Perfect Phrases to Recognize Effort

As Dynamic Leaders we acknowledge efforts as well as results.

- Thank you for keeping at this.
- The hardest time to keep going is when the fog is thick and the shore isn't visible. Even then, you kept moving. Thanks!
- It has been said that 80 percent of success is just showing up. You have that one down.
- Some people show up but aren't really there. You show up all the way. Thanks!
- That may not have been the result you wanted, but it shows you're stretching.
- Are you as impressed as I am with your ability to keep going forward? Where did you find the endurance? It was courageous and inspiring. Thanks!

- → It takes more than great ideas to lead. It takes sustained effort. You've proven that ability.
- → I can think of about a hundred points in the road where someone else would have given up. You kept going.
- → You could have left the new road for a more beaten path. You didn't do that—you kept going. That shows the endurance a leader needs.
- → You're one *no* closer to a *yes*. The fact that you don't let the nos stop you shows great effort.
- → If it were easy, everyone would do it. It wasn't, which is why you stand alone in that action.
- → I'm enjoying singing your praises. What else are you working on that I need to recognize?

Perfect Phrases to Recognize Progress and to Celebrate Milestones

These phrases acknowledge all forms of progress. When we note progress, we reinforce it because whatever we put attention on grows.

- → Let's all note the excellent progress we made since ___________.
- → Let's contrast that to a year ago when you ___________.
- → Where do you see the greatest progress in this initiative?

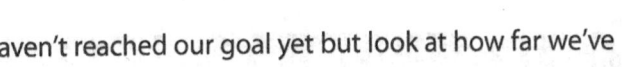

- We haven't reached our goal yet but look at how far we've come.
- Let's stop for a moment and see how far we've come.
- Do you realize where you are and how far you've come?
- If the goal looks far off to you now, look in the rearview mirror to see how much closer you are to the goal than when you started.
- You may not have developed in the area of __________ as you imagined, but I'd say that's because you've been doing deep foundational work instead of patching cracks in the wall.
- We're not there yet, but we're way closer.
- You/We reached a real milestone by __________.
- What do you think is a suitable way to celebrate this milestone?
- This is a milestone for you and for our leader development process.
- Do you realize what a milestone this is?
- We can talk about the future and where we go from here later. Right now, I want to acknowledge what a milestone this is.
- Is there a milestone we've reached that I haven't recognized yet?

Perfect Phrases to Acknowledge Developing Leaders' Achieving Autonomy

Once emerging leaders develop autonomy, the best reinforcement we can offer is to talk to them as Dynamic Leader peers. If we congratulate them or tell them about how well they are doing, but give counsel and never invite it, the message is: "I'm telling you you've arrived, but I don't really believe it myself." These phrases don't just tell, they show your Dynamic Leaders you do see their genius.

- Collaborate with me on a problem I'm facing.
- The way you handled that makes me want to ask for input on a situation I'm faced with now.
- I trust you completely on the _______ (project, initiative). I invite you to share the details so I can learn from how you handle it. And if you'd like to share ideas, pose problems, ask for help or collaboration, or dialogue as peers, I'm in.
- That was brilliant! Teach me your process (philosophy).
- How did you come to that conclusion?
- What did you learn from this experience that I should know?
- Clearly you've become an expert in _________.
- Have you considered submitting an article on this project (experience) to _________ (appropriate trade journal)?

- We're having a conference that can benefit from hearing about your project.
- This was an amazing accomplishment. Let's issue a press release on it.
- I'll share what I have learned from you during this relationship. You taught me __________.

CHAPTER 13

Perfect Phrases to Enlist Organizational Support for Leader Development and Succession Planning

A Dynamic Leader enlists organizational support for leader development and succession planning so organizations stay competitive and continue to flourish even after he or she is gone. This chapter takes the leadership development process beyond individual guidance and into creating a culture where succession planning is a given and leaders at all levels are valued and cultivated.

There are plenty of compelling reasons why it is in an organization's interest to take leadership development seriously. These phrases help us communicate those benefits.

Perfect Phrases to Tie Leadership Development into Succession Planning

Succession planning is an important motivation for Dynamic Leader development programs. While it's important not to promise a future we can't guarantee, preparing an emerging leader to replace someone should that person retire or leave creates a focus for the leader development process.

- → How do you think we should plan for succession in the area of ___________? Be specific.
- → What positions do you see as particularly sensitive should we lose _______ (a leader)?
- → We want to develop your expertise in the area of _______ to ensure continuity if an existing leader needs a replacement.
- → If you can think like the CEO of your area of influence, it will help you think like the CEO of the larger organization.
- → Let's imagine you were a candidate to replace the leadership position in your area. Let's go through the qualities, experience, and skills you would need to fill those shoes. Then, let's create a plan for you to develop those traits.
- → We're focusing on the skills you can use where you are now, but also on the skills you would need to qualify to step up should we need to fill a leadership position in _______ area.
- → I don't know if you have CEO (other senior leadership title) in your future, but if it's a possibility, I'd like to do what we can to build the knowledge and experiences you would need.

- Let's imagine you were going to replace the leadership team in your area. What qualities, experience, and skills would your replacement need to fill your shoes? Then, let's create a plan for you to develop your replacement.

Perfect Phrases to Encourage Others to Develop New Leaders at All Levels

These phrases encourage emerging leaders to develop other leaders and prepare for the possibility of their own departures.

- I think of you as a truly Dynamic Leader. Are you teaching others what you know and how to do what you do?
- If we're going to leave any kind of legacy, it is important for you to develop leaders at all levels.
- Should something happen that would cause you to leave, who do you think is responsible for preparing a replacement for you?
- Unless you already have a succession plan for yourself, I believe you need to start one now.
- If you left suddenly, would there be a leadership vacuum?
- What have you done to make sure you have someone ready to replace you when it's time for you to move on?
- If you don't have a plan to have someone ready to replace you should there be a need, what can you do starting now to do get someone prepared?
- I've learned so much from you. I'd like to see you share what you know with others.

- I think others could benefit from learning about how you developed your leadership style.
- I read about CEOs who invite senior leaders—one at time—to spend weekends with them. Everyone learns a lot from the conversations. Could you imagine doing that?
- Our newer leaders could really benefit from having conversations that challenge and encourage them as they develop. I suggest you meet one-on-one with a couple of emerging leaders.
- If you left suddenly, is there anyone who could carry on your legacy? Are you preparing someone?
- You don't seem interested in succession. Have we done something to lose your loyalty?

Perfect Phrases to Generate Support for Dynamic Leader Development by Sharing Your Own Experience with Other Leaders

These phrases share personal experiences of the value of leader development. They can be used to inspire others to champion leader development and succession planning.

- I can go on vacation for two weeks without anyone calling me because of the leader development work we've done.
- At first I wasn't sure I had the time to help others develop their leadership qualities. I discovered I'm getting as much out of it as they are.
- Developing leaders has dynamized my experience here. It's crystallized my own understanding of what it takes to

lead successfully, and it has added meaning to everything I've been doing over the years.

- I need to tell you what incredible resources my emerging leaders have become for me.
- My emerging leader took what I taught her and threw it back at me when I was ready to make an ill-advised decision. What an asset that was!
- Every time I meet with my emerging leader, the possibilities unfold.
- I had no idea what a difference it would make for me to have people who have developed as leaders. I don't have to do everything myself anymore.
- I just got back from a meeting with a group of leaders I've developed. They're brilliant, and it was exhilarating.

Perfect Phrases to Get Your Organization Focused on Clearing Barriers to Leader Development

Your individual efforts at succession planning may run into bureaucratic obstacles within your organization. These phrases encourage the removal of these hierarchal limitations.

- Our emerging leaders are limited by the ways we guard information. We need to increase access to information by __________.
- We missed an opportunity to __________ because of the information hierarchy. By the time questions got passed

up the ladder and answers were passed down, we lost an opportunity. To keep this from happening I recommend we __________.

- → We need our intranet to be a genuine source of empowerment and information so our lower level leaders can lead without having to run everything by us.
- → If we think we're in control of this organization, we're not listening. Let's not kid ourselves into thinking we can control everything that happens at every level. Let's give the people who are on the front lines the tools they need to be able to lead from where they are.
- → If our managers can't lead in situations like __________ and call audibles, we're cutting them off at the knees. We need to take the shackles off of them and empower them to act.

Perfect Phrases to Get Your Organization Focused on Succession Planning and Development

Leader development can take the form of planned and structured job rotations, relationships with mentors and coaches, and exposure to new challenges, as well as formal education and development. These phrases launch conversations about development.

- We need to think about how we are preparing today's frontline employees to lead in the future.
- Online performance support and peer-to-peer networking and resource sharing is replacing corporate universities, and we need to get with it.
- We have a lot of boomers in leadership positions, and I'm worried about what will happen when they retire.
- If we treat our employees like disposable resources, they won't have the loyalty to care about succession planning. Investing in leadership development is an investment in loyalty and our future.
- When I think about how ________ (company) declined since ________ left, I worry about our own succession planning.
- Everyone thought ________ was a great leader, but when he/she left, the company declined. That makes me think he/she wasn't that great a leader after all.
- The best companies are deliberate about building a leadership culture. I think we can be one of the best.
- What would happen if we extended our succession planning to all levels of the organization, not just the senior ones?
- I question whether we have the leadership bench strength we'll need for the next five to ten years. Even companies that have historically been well-known for creating leaders are reevaluating their approaches and experimenting with new ideas.

- Are we helping our evolving leaders develop a greater awareness of other worldviews?
- Do we have the talent we need to move into new markets now? What about three to five years from now? I'm not sure we do.
- Successful leaders leave functioning organizations behind them.
- What is our leadership brand? Do we have one?
- We need people in place who know how to connect and communicate, rather than command.
- We need to develop leaders who generate commitment, not compliance.
- We could count on individual leaders to initiate mentoring and coaching, or we could organize a more formal program.
- I want to organize a meeting to kick off a leadership development initiative.
- I'm picturing us working together to create a sustainable community of people who can probe and challenge our emergent leaders' assumptions and practices and provide support along the way.
- Having a reputation for developing leaders would attract the best talent from business schools, colleges, and other companies.

Appendix A

Dynamic Leadership Index

Establish a baseline and monitor your progress. Rate yourself and your emerging leaders on the following items using a scale of 1–5, with 1 indicating "needs improvement" and 5 indicating "excellent." For added benefit, include an example to illustrate each score.

Note: 5 does not mean perfect. However, if an emerging leader is strong in an area but still could use improvement, a score of 4 gives room to reflect improvement. For low scores, seek guidance in the corresponding section of the main text.

You can find a more detailed index online at: www.speakstrong.com/leaderinventory/. Use it as a baseline to evaluate progress.

A Dynamic Leader is someone who . . .

1. Takes responsibility and avoids blame
2. Is trustworthy and works to increase trust in the organization
3. Puts the needs of the organization, its customers, and its people ahead of his or her own quest for personal power

4. Consistently works according to pro-social values
5. Uses influence and empowerment instead of power games and pressure
6. Integrates information into a unique, developed point of view
7. Empowers others more by engaging with them on a high level than by instruction
8. Addresses obstacles as they arise
9. Knows when to lead, when to manage, and when to stand down
10. Knows where a developing leader is in the development process and engages at the appropriate level
11. Has a clear leadership philosophy and the ability to share it with others
12. Is open to receiving mentoring, coaching, and input from people at all levels
13. Uses Beginner's Mind to obtain a fresh perspective
14. Encourages Beginner's Mind in others
15. Looks for opportunities in problems
16. Guides others to look for opportunities in problems
17. Innovates and takes charge as situations indicate whether "leader" is in his or her title or not
18. Empowers others to take charge to the maximum level of their abilities
19. Measures leadership skills by the ability to empower others
20. Sees leadership development as a lifelong process
21. Understands the difference between leading and managing, and balances the two functions

22. Operates at an optimal level of empowerment
23. Works with enthusiasm
24. Inspires enthusiasm in others
25. Works in alignment with others
26. Creates alignment in work groups and with associates
27. Elicits and incorporates input from work groups and associates
28. Communicates from head, heart, and will
29. Creates and communicates momentum
30. Balances grace and assertiveness in communication
31. Balances inquiry and advocacy
32. Engages in dialogue before decree
33. Understands and optimizes his or her leadership style
34. Helps other to understand and optimize their leadership styles
35. Embraces the (emerging) leadership role
36. Has a dynamic and developed leadership philosophy
37. Meets or renegotiates agreements and expectations
38. Follows through
39. Holds others accountable for following through
40. Shares skills and insights with leaders at all levels
41. Is committed to leader development, and supports the success of team members, employees, and other associates
42. Communicates clearly, consistently, and eloquently
43. Understands mission, vision, and values
44. Works in alignment with mission, vision, and values
45. Works in alignment with associates at all levels

46. Demonstrates creative thinking
47. Has innovative ideas
48. Uses appropriate criteria to make decisions
49. Coordinates innovation with existing obligations
50. Thinks and speaks imaginatively
51. Thinks and speaks strategically
52. Avoids victim language
53. Speaks like a leader rather than a follower
54. Illustrates points in compelling language
55. Expands thinking beyond existing norms
56. Increases autonomy level for others
57. Is willing to challenge the status quo
58. Is willing to act outside of comfort zone (or, has a huge comfort zone)
59. Makes ideas practical
60. Brainstorms effectively
61. Is willing to challenge opinions
62. Takes ownership of problems
63. Is resourceful
64. Sees beyond binary thinking and false dichotomies
65. Supports leadership development in the organization
66. Knows and uses information resources dynamically
67. Makes timely decisions with adequate information
68. Learns from all experiences
69. Gives useful feedback and suggestions to mentors and colleagues

Appendix B

Leader Development Checklist

This checklist keeps us on track as we develop emerging leaders. When you develop a leader at any level, remember to:

1. Model Dynamic Leadership.
2. Commit completely to the development of your emerging leaders.
3. Have and clearly communicate your personal leadership philosophy.
4. Keep the vision of the future current and inspiring.
5. Acknowledge displays of leadership.
6. Draw out emerging leader's point of view.
7. Be trustworthy, and increase trust.
8. Act with integrity.
9. Consistently act from pro-social values, especially when it is most difficult. Expect the same of others.

10. Recognize courage, and provide feedback if it is lacking.
11. Make it safe for emerging leaders to address issues and share ideas.
12. Ask for feedback regarding your performance.
13. Speak up when you suspect an emerging leader is holding back.
14. Listen.
15. Treat an emerging leader as a peer.
16. Encourage an emerging leader to take on projects that expand potential.
17. Support an emerging leader's decisions.
18. Stand back and let emerging leaders act autonomously when appropriate.
19. Give tough feedback when needed with emphasis on what you want over what you don't want.
20. Put your own ego on hold. Remain authentically humble.
21. Celebrate emerging leaders' successes with the same enthusiasm that you celebrate your own.
22. Allow yourself to be influenced by your emerging leaders.
23. Trade your own use of power for influence.
24. Have fun.

Appendix C

The Leadership-Management Distinction

As noted in Chapter 1, the leadership-management distinction is a source of a great deal of confusion. While Dynamic Leaders need to have both management and leadership skills, it is useful to distinguish between them. This list focuses on leadership and management *activities* instead of roles.

- We lead when we set a direction. We manage when we carry that direction out.
- We lead when we work with ideas and people. We manage when we work with processes for people to implement.
- We lead when we create a vision. We manage when we create a plan.
- We lead when we inspire others. We manage when we provide structure.

- We lead when we envision, propose, and create change. We manage when we organize how the change will be implemented.
- We lead when we see what could be. We manage when we deliver what is and what leadership decided will be.
- We lead when we originate initiatives. We manage when we make the initiatives happen.
- We lead when we develop other leaders. We manage when we take action to make sure the Dynamic Leader development process moves smoothly.

About the Authors

Meryl Runion, CSP, brings her management communication authorship, her experience training emergent leaders, and her experience working with the military to develop mentoring training and leadership succession programs to this book. She is a Certified Speaking Professional and the author of six books that have sold more than a quarter million copies worldwide. She also loves to hike, learn, dance, and find better ways to say things.

Meryl works with leaders at every level who have moved beyond victimhood and power games and are ready to develop their magnetic influence based on confluent communication and reciprocal engagement. She offers Dynamic Leader Certification.

You can contact Meryl at:

- Twitter: http://twitter.com/MerylRunion
- LinkedIn: http://www.linkedin.com/in/speakstrong
- Website: http://www.speakstrong.com
- Leadership Development Online Training: http://www.speakstrong.com/teleseminars/
- Leadership Articles: http://www.speakstrong.com/articles/
- Leadership Development Index: www.speakstrong.com/leaderinventory/

Wendy Mack is a nationally recognized speaker, consultant, and thought leader who advises leaders on how to mobilize energy for change. Since founding T3 Consulting in 2001, Wendy has consulted with dozens of companies on the engagement and communication aspects of their change initiatives. Wendy is also the author of numerous books and articles on the topics of change, communication, and leadership. Her keynotes and workshops and have helped more than 20,000 leaders develop the skills to engage, align, and motivate employees.

You can contact Wendy at:

- Twitter: http://twitter.com/Wendy_Mack
- LinkedIn: http://www.linkedin.com/in/wendymack
- Website: http://www.WendyMack.com
- Leadership Development Workshops: http://wendymack.com/workshops.html
- Free Articles: http://wendymack.com/resource-center/library.html
- Free e-books: http://wendymack.com/resource-center/ebooks.html

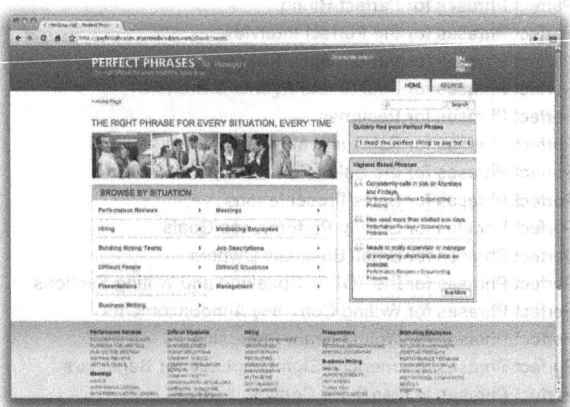